INTELLECTUAL
SCHIZOPHRENIA

INTERNATIONAL LIBRARY OF PHILOSOPHY
AND THEOLOGY
Philosophical and Historical Studies

INTELLECTUAL
SCHIZOPHRENIA

*Culture, Crisis
and Education*

ROUSAS J. RUSHDOONY

Preface by Edmund A. Opitz

PRESBYTERIAN AND REFORMED PUBLISHING CO.
Phillipsburg, New Jersey
1980

Library of Congress Catalog Card Number 61-11011

Printed in the United States of America

ISBN: 0-87552-411-7

*To Dr. Gilbert den Dulk
and to the memory
of Mrs. Gilbert den Dulk
True and Able Champions of Education
and the Continuing Reformation*

Publisher's Note

Intellectual Schizophrenia is one of a series of "Philosophical and Historical Studies" written for the International Library of Philosophy and Theology. These studies will stress the rethinking of philosophy and historiography as well as history in terms of a radical presuppositionalism, while also presenting important analyses of contemporary thought from other perspectives. The premises of contemporary thought involve unrecognized religious presuppositions which, by conditioning the concepts of fact and history, lead to alien results. While all the studies will be in the perspective of the Reformed faith, most will thus be further governed by the developed presuppositionalism of modern Calvinists. Rousas J. Rushdoony is the editor of this series.

The Presbyterian and Reformed Publishing Company, which in cooperation with the Baker Book House has already introduced such stimulating thinkers of this philosophy, such as Herman Dooyeweerd (*A New Critique of Theoretical Thought* and *In the Twilight of Western Thought*), J. M. Spier (*An Introduction to Christian Philosophy* and *Christianity and Existentialism*), H. Van Riessen (*The Society of the Future* and *Nietzsche*) R. J. Rushdoony (*By What Standard?*), Henry Van Til (*The Calvinistic Concept of Culture*), and Cornelius Van Til (*The New Modernism* and *The Defense of the Faith*) now makes available in this series, together with other works, important studies from this major school of thought.

Other series in the International Library of Philosophy and Theology

include the *Modern Thinkers Series* edited by Dr. David H. Freeman
of the Philosophy Department of Rhode Island University and the
Biblical and Theological Studies series edited by J. Marcellus Kik,
former associate editor of *Christianity Today*.

Charles H. Craig, *Director*

Table of Contents

Preface

The purpose of this study has not been either the criticism or praise of the schools as such, but the understanding of the schools and their basic philosophy as cultural manifestations. The era now rapidly drawing to an end has had, as one of its most characteristic cultural products and agencies, the state-sponsored school. An assessment of the school's role, a criticism and some appreciation of it, has been attempted. In most civilizations, the intimations of immortality are an essential part of the cultural experience. It is believed that man has finally arrived, and the true and final forms of expression at last manifested; only development and fulfilment remains, and a change of premises is seen as anarchy or chaos. In the temper of modernity especially, men are more apt to believe "wisdom was born with us" than to reckon soberly that "wisdom may die with us," or at our hands. An examination of premises is therefore of paramount importance in terms of future potentialities. The state schools and their philosophy are decisive and important aspects of a now faltering and waning culture, and they are a very present power. As long as their culture endures, they will endure and prosper, but they cannot outlast their particular premises and culture.

Accordingly, this writer has no quarrel with those who work for the furtherance or "improvement" of the state schools, or teach therein, nor with the critics of these schools. The intended perspective is cultural rather than intercedent. Most certainly, a person should not be buried before his death, but neither should his immortality be presumed because of his present survival. The signs of a coming change of cultural premises must be recognized, but the present realities must still be lived with. Man cannot live as a creature of tomorrow, but to be bound by the present is to live in terms of past victories and present defeats.

Portions of this book were first delivered as lectures to the Christian Teachers' Association of the Northwest on October 15 and 16, 1959, at Lynden, Washington. The Board of Directors of the Association, without implying agreement, felt the lectures of sufficient relevance to merit wider attention and debate, and they accordingly requested their publication. The lectures were, as a result, expanded to include issues developed in discussions, smaller gatherings, and correspondence.

The author is indebted to Principal and Mrs. Mark Vander Ark of Lynden for their gracious hospitality, and their congeniality to the discussions in their home that extended beyond midnight. William N. Blake, then president of the Association, gave every kindness and help possible to the author, and graciously provided specific data regarding Christian schools.

A more personal note is necessary. I believe in the necessity of more emphasis on education and scholarship, but, especially within the institutional church, no greater tragedy characterizes the current scene, especially in the United States, than the retreat of scholarship from the pulpit to the school. Accordingly, in the last two centuries, Christian scholarship, theology and philosophy have been academic in their orientation. Such an orientation is definitely necessary, but the vitality and relevance of Christian thought has been largely lost. It is significant that the modern Calvinist re-awakening stems from Abraham Kuyper, very definitely a man actively linked with the problems and life of his day. I have accordingly believed that the pulpit is the place for Christian scholarship and philosophy. In that faith, I have been actively supported and furthered by the members and officers of the Orthodox Presbyterian Church of Santa Cruz, California, and for their love, prayers and support I am deeply grateful.

Two of the appendices, "Academic Freedom" and "The Menace of the Sunday School," first appeared in *Torch and Trumpet*, the publication of the Reformed Fellowship.

R. J. R.

Santa Cruz, California

Introduction

Mr. Rushdoony has written a trenchant, compact, and uncompromising Christian response to the cultural crisis. This book is the work of a vigorous, independent and logical mind. No reader's toes, I dare say, will remain wholly untrampled—which is precisely what we should demand of a writer who professes to "speak to our condition."

The crisis of our culture comes into one of its focal points in education, and this is the author's point of entry into the problem. It is a contention of this book that education, in the fullest sense of the word, is inescapably, Christian education. The term "secular education," in the author's view, brings together ideas which are at least anomalous, if not downright contradictory. Mr. Rushdoony, it is obvious from this arresting assertion, does not here offer just one more amiable discussion about conditions in our schools. His book is a trenchant criticism of contemporary educational theory and practice, whose shortcomings he measures against the demands of the Christian revelation.

Culture is religion externalized, and our culture bears the imprints of its molding by Christianity; we were Christendom before we began thinking of ourselves as Europe or The West. The hallmarks of this faith stamp themselves even on our rebellion against it for every rejection or denial implies something positive against which the reaction occurs. The positive things in our culture have been Christian things, or the things of Christian cultivation. T. S. Eliot has said somewhat the same thing in *The Idea of a Christian Society*. There are some, he observes, who say, "that a society has ceased to be Christian when religious practices have been abandoned, when behavior ceases to be regulated by reference to Christian principle . . ." But there is another way of looking at the matter. "The other point of view, which is less readily apprehended, is that a society has not ceased to be Christian until it has become positively something else. It is my contention that we have to-day a culture which is mainly negative, but which, so far as it is positive, is still Christian. I do not think that it can remain negative, because a negative culture has ceased to be efficient in a world where economic as well as spiritual forces are proving the efficiency of cultures which, even when pagan, are positive; and I believe that the choice before us is between the formation of a new Christian culture, and the acceptance of a pagan one." (London, 1939, p. 13)

The word "pagan" usually connotes an innocent, carefree child of nature. This kind of thing is hardly a live option for modern man and, presumably, is not what Eliot has in mind. Christianity's chief antagonist for the past two centuries has been the secular faith of the Enlightenment, and a perverse form of it is the main contender today. In its early phases there was something attractive about this faith, but in its reactionary phase during this century it has spawned an idolatrous, statist cult manifesting itself now as Communism, and again as various dilutions of Marxism.

Communism is one version of environmentalism—the notion that a man's character is made for him and not by him. Improve his material circumstances and you change man for the better. Education, under this dispensation, is the sum total of efforts to adapt man to his surroundings.

Should the educated man be adjusted to his environment? Adjustment is the aim, as many educationists see it. Some of them narrow the concept of the environment down to the social group and recommend that schooling be a process of merging the man into the mass. These theories have not gone unchallenged. Man, say the opponents of environmentalism, has the capacity to respond creatively to his environment and surpass it. And the group, they point out, may exhibit norms that are warped or vicious. Accommodation to these is debasing. The environmentalists return to the fray by asking their critics if the aim of education, then, is to produce maladjusted products? It is not, obviously, but at this point the argument runs aground because both parties accept too limiting a notion of what constitutes man's environment. As the term is commonly used, environment refers to the world of time and space, the world of things, the physical frame within which man struggles to survive. No Christian can accept so narrow a definition of environment; his natural habitat is the universe of time and space, but he is also environed by another dimension, eternity.

This dimension has dropped out of contemporary life. The modern outlook does not include it, with the result that multitudes of people no longer feel a sense of life as participation in a cosmic adventure. They have come to believe that the world of things which can be seen, felt, measured and tested is man's sole habitat. Belief in the reality of things not seen has dimmed or disappeared and we are living, so the French writer André Malraux tells us, in "the first agnostic civilization." This charge, or description, is all too true. It is a fundamental assumption, unconsciously presupposed in our time—and thus more a mood than a premise—that man is a creature of the natural order only. It was the evil genius of Karl Marx to seize upon this mood and make it explicit. Communism today offers a godless religion and a this-worldly salvation, a caricature or parody, point by point, of Christianity. And one has the uneasy feeling that many people, now on the fence, would go Communist except for an inertia which prevents them from following their premises to the bitter end.

We are living, some have suggested, in the post-Christian era. Our outlook is, in general, man-centered, secularist, and utopian. It is materialistic and rationalistic. It uses majority decision as its criterion of right. It asserts a false individualism as against natural associations such as the family and intimate communty groupings, and then it turns to nationalism as the principle of social cohesion. There are very few new truths, but there are always lots of new errors—and these are some which have gained acceptance during recent centuries. The axioms now widely taken for granted are largely 18th and 19th century products, and they are alien to the Christian and humanist tradition. But even though they seem more deeply entrenched than ever in the popular mentality, they have already come under fire from some of the more discerning minds.

The acids of modernity may have eaten away at historic Christianity, but more recently they have also attacked the Enlightenment faith. Christianity has been purged of some undesirable accretions during the ordeal, but its rival has probably been damaged beyond repair. Reflect further on some of the tenets of the latter and ask Where are now its votaries? Futurism, the gospel of unimaginable progress; Scientism, belief in the messianic potential of science; Democracy, faith in the omniscience of majorities; Socialism, utopia by means of political ownership—who now defends these dogmas? They still have their partisans, true, but they gain few recruits. Christianity, on the other hand, is resurgent; not always wisely so, perhaps, but it is, at any rate, alive enough to challenge the ablest contemporary minds. It fared badly under the shallow optimism which reigned last century because Christianity is a religion of hard answers. It is not called into play when men are content with glib answers to soft questions; it partakes of the tragic view of life. Henry Adams ironically remarked that his contemporaries had "solved the universe." Christianity is not for the likes of these. But today's crisis is religion's opportunity. Life again confronts men with paradox, uncertainty, dilemma and catastrophe; the smooth facade is dented and breached. Man tries to play God and fails to secure even a niche for himself in any pantheon. The homemade heaven he tries to fashion on earth—in totalitarian lands—resembles an old-fashioned hell. He aspires to the role of deity and reverts to subhumanity. Perhaps if men attempt a more modest role—to become truly human—we may, with God's help, make it. But such a choice as this demands an individual commitment. Before we seek for better answers, let alone hard answers, we must start to ask the right questions. In this respect each of us needs all the help he can get, and he can get help from the right books—such as the present volume.

This book will not find favor with professional educationists, nor with those who reject the author's religion. But even many churchmen, regrettably, are more at home with sentimentality than hard, rigorous thinking. They will be uncomfortable with the way this book challenges them to re-examine things they have taken for granted. Many churchmen are disturbed because the Bible may no longer be read in the so-called public schools, but how many acknowledge the inevitability of the secularist trend in tax supported and politically controlled schools? The state is secular, in a free society, the alternative being some form of caesaropapism. It follows that wherever government gets into the education business—whether at local or national levels— its influence will tend to secularize the schools. The churches respond to this challenge by offering released time religious instruction, and by establishing—at a progressive rate—their own weekday schools. Laudable as are these efforts, it is feared that, in all too many cases, parochial and private schools operate with the same theories of education as tax supported institutions. Hence the importance of the present book, a penetrating, closely reasoned study, which starts from Christian premises and exhibits an easy familiarity with the vagaries of current educational theory.

Mr. Rushdoony espouses a biblical faith based on a consistent and rigorous Calvinism. Does this lessen the value of his book for those who come from other traditions within Christendom? Not at all, in my judgment—speaking as one whose ties are with the traditions of liberal Congregationalism. I'm not sure that I see eye to eye with Mr. Rushdoony on every point, and I might employ a different vocabulary in places, but basically we both speak the same language. Doctrinal differences, in short, are compatible with dogmatic accord.

Before we can discuss the nature of education intelligently we must have come to some understanding of the nature of man. Soviet schooling, with its emphasis on scientific and technological instruction, reflects the Marxian understanding of human nature. Whatever else we say about the Marxian view of man, we must certainly admit that it falls short in every dimension of the Christian view of man—a creature created by God for fellowship with Himself. If the Christian view of man's nature and destiny is our premise, we cannot possibly agree that even a superbly trained engineer is a finished educational product. We need lots of engineers in modern society, and good ones are to be preferred to those less highly skilled. But engineering is in the realm of means, and the crucial question concerns the ends to be served by these means. It's fine that we constantly improve our means, but unless we simultaneously improve our ends we generate a conflict by hitching too much power to too little purpose. "Power is never a good," Alfred the Great observed, "except he be good that has it." It would further the interests of clarity if we could use the word training to describe the instruction that has to do with means, or instrumental knowledge; reserving the word education for that which has to do with ends, or formative knowledge.

Instruction in instrumental knowledge is not education, although it is part of education and useful in its own right. It is needful that men possess such skills as the ability to lay bricks, cut hair, add figures, perform experiments in physics and chemistry, write books and preach sermons. But while the possession of such skills is desirable and important, their exercise is not the distinctive mark of an educated man. It is true, however, that an educated man ought to have a quiverful of such and similar talents and be able, like Jefferson, "to calculate an eclipse, survey an estate, tie an artery, plan an edifice, try a cause, break a horse, dance a minuet and play the violin." But this is merely to say that a man ought to be trained as well as educated.

The so-called public school system in the United States stems mainly from the 19th century and partakes of the dubious philosophy of that time and subsequent periods. As a system of instruction supported by taxation and compelling attendance it was bound to veer toward secularism and statism, but other inherent defects were apparent as well. Late last century the astute French critic, Ernest Renan observed that "countries which, like the United States, have set up considerable popular instruction without any serious higher education, will long have to expiate their error by their intellectual mediocrity, the vulgarity of their manners, their superficial spirit, their failure in general intelligence." (Quoted by Albert Jay Nock, *The Theory of Education in the United States,* 1932, 1949, Chicago, p. 20)

In the twentieth century, compulsory government schooling got its philosopher, John Dewey. "The educational process," as viewed by this influential teacher, "has no end beyond itself." Education is "vital energy seeking opportunity for effective exercise." (John Dewey, *Democracy and Education,* N.Y. 1921, p. 59 and p. 84) The Dewey philosophy is pragmatic, experimental and instrumentalist—not advanced tentatively for argument and debate, but insisted upon dogmatically as the only permissible point of view. I. L. Kandel, Professor of Education, Emeritus, Teachers' College, Columbia University, writes, in "School and Society" for August 22, 1953, "The critic, however sincere, who ventures to comment adversely on the consequences of the cult of pragmatism, experimentalism, or instrumentalism is regarded as almost committing sacrilege."

But now it is admitted on all sides that the sacred cow is out of sorts. There is something wrong with our system of education because there is something wrong with our theory of education, and we won't correct our system until we straighten out our theory. But this we cannot even begin to do unless we know what is normative. We really do know, as a matter of fact, but we need to be reminded that the norms are Christian imperatives. It is Mr. Rushdoony's accomplishment to remind us in terms we are not likely to forget.

Rev. Edmund A. Opitz
Foundation for Economic Education
Irvington-on-Hudson, N.Y.

October 28, 1960

1

The School and the Whole Person

Contemporary educational theorists have much to say about educating the whole child and dealing with the total needs of the person. Theoretically, it seems a most desirable process, but, on reflection, both the goal and the process appear to have very dangerous implications. Consider, for example, this comment by Helmut Schoeck:

> Last year I had a talk with the director of teacher education in one of our universities. This jovial gentleman confided his greatest worry to me: "You know, our graduates, after four years of indoctrination in our program, go out from here with pretty much the same attitudes they had when they came as freshmen. I really think we ought to get permission to electro-shock them."[1]

While too much cannot be read into this observation, neither can it be by-passed. The remark Schoeck quotes is after all a common one, its equivalent heard on many a college campus. Whether

[1] Helmut Schoeck, "Individuality vs. Equality" in Felix Morley, ed.: *Essays on Individuality*, p. 124. Phila.: U. of Penna. Press, 1958.

1

stated facetiously or with an irritable weariness, it does betray
a concept of education which is rarely recognized as basic to
the modern mind.

To understand modern educational theory, it is important to
recognize the impact of John Locke. Locke's influence was two-
fold, both as an educational theorist, and as the founder of
modern psychology, through which he has had a continuing influence. It was important to Locke, as a zealous champion of the
Enlightenment and a forerunner of Empiricism, to eliminate the
effect of the past and wipe out any concept of the mind that
would leave innate ideas or any stock of ideas to the individual.
Accordingly, he gave to the Enlightenment its ideal weapon
against God and the past, the concept of the mind as a blank
piece of white paper. Although not entirely new, the idea received its influential formulation from Locke. The mind begins
life without any burden from the past; it is like a white paper
without any markings. All its ideas are empirically aroused; the
mind is free, and nothing can exist in it that is not first in the
senses. Thus, the mind cannot create ideas; they are received as
impressions, then compounded and translated. The mind is thus
essentially passive and receptive, although Locke at times speaks
of it, contradictorily, as active and free. The essential passivity
of the mind is apparent in that no true explanation of the Self
was possible for Locke; it was simply an "internal, infallible perception that we are," an unexplained and soon eroded concept
in later thinking of the Enlightenment.

The marvels of this theory for educators of the Enlightenment
are immediately apparent. Man was able to remake man and the
educator to play the role of a god. The hated and despised past
could be cancelled out and man be given in effect a new inheritance. No modern goal in education is understandable except
in terms of this hope of the Enlightenment. Education thus involved a war against the past, and two of the most monstrous
aspects of man's past were Calvinism and Scholasticism, against
which all men of intellect must make war. For the Enlightenment

"education" became a veritable mania, a magical concept which was the cure-all for all problems—social, ethical, and economic. Education would produce universal brotherhood and a paradise on earth, freedom and happiness for all. Pestalozzi translated much of this into practice with his educational techniques and methods. Lessing, Herder and others attacked patriotism in the name of cosmopolitanism; all lesser divisions than the world were frowned upon. A thing to be true had to be universal and valid for all men. An 'aristocratic' concept such as predestination was untenable. Authority and tradition were inevitably wrong, and rebellion against them the duty of intelligence. Accordingly, the static (as universal) and the rational (as against the realistic) were exalted and made basic to all human activity and philosophy. In terms of this the Enlightenment developed also the concept of 'necessary' ideas, things necessary in and of themselves.

Not every facet of the Enlightenment is of importance to us in this context. The concept of the mind as a clean tablet was very quickly exploded as a psychological reality but it remained as an *ideal*. It became the ideal concept undergirding *the idea of revolution*. History was to be wiped out by revolution, a clean tablet effected, and history begun anew. This concept dominated all thinking in the French Revolution and extended itself to the point of beginning again in the reckoning of time. It was basic to the thinking of the anarchists, Marxists such as Lenin and others, and still underwrites all revolutionary expectancy and post-revolutionary cynicism. It has been basic to all Utopian thinking.[2]

Again, it has provided the ideal for *scientific thinking*. The true scientist ostensibly wipes his mind free of all preconceptions and approaches his subject with a clean-tablet mind, ready to see and interpret the facts in and of themselves. This scientific attitude is one of the great myths of modern times. That the scientist actually approaches his subject with a variety of axioms of thought and pre-theoretical and religious presuppositions, Her-

[2] See R. L. Bruckberger: *Image of America*. New York: Viking, 1959.

man Dooyeweerd and Cornelius Van Til have amply shown.[3] His clean-tablet mind is actually free only of the attitudes the Enlightenment rebelled against, preconceptions being identified with Calvinism and Scholasticism. *Instrumentalism* is another expression of the same basic concept and assumes that it alone possesses the ability to attain true knowledge because it alone is ostensibly free of preconceived ideas in approaching factuality. This is again a mythical faith, and an impossibility. The instrumentalist also is guilty of extensive and basically religious presuppositions which provide the unconscious axioms of all his thinking.

But, more pertinent to our concern, the clean tablet concept has become *the* educational ideal. True education involves a ruthless wiping of the slate, cleaning it of all roots in the past and of all ideas and opinions not derived from the educational process. Indeed, some professors self-consciously and conscientiously employ a kind of shock therapy designed to jolt the student out of all preconceptions, wean him from the past, home, nation, and religion, in order that the student can now truly pursue knowledge. The electroshock therapy idea is thus a fitting image for the clean tablet concept of education, and it is no wonder that more than one educator has ruefully considered it!

As a result, the characteristic pattern of modern education becomes understandable, as does also the hostility of many people to education. Education, in aiming at a clean tablet as the first step towards true education, is inevitably productive of a radical rootlessness in the intelligentsia. And this, in the small town and rural areas where roots are often deepest, is strongly resented. The young man who went off to school with deep roots returns contemptuous of roots. The intellectual refuses to acknowledge

[3] For Dooyeweerd, see *A New Critique of Theoretical Thought*, 4 v. and *In The Twilight of Western Thought, Studies in the Pretended Autonomy of Philosophical Thought*. For Van Til, see *The New Modernism, The Defense of the Faith, The Metaphysics of Apologetics, A Christian Theory of Knowledge*. All published by The Presbyterian and Reformed Publishing Co., Philadelphia, Penna.

the validity of the simplest conclusion unless it has been tested and established by his own processes. Accordingly, as long as there is any cultural vitality, there will be a strong resentment against such education. Only when such education has completely eroded all the cultural watersheds will the resentment disappear, only to give way to the deluge. Indeed, the resistance of many students to contemporary education is sometimes an indication of mental and cultural health. Such education is an unceasing war of attrition on all cultures and brooks no terms, demanding unconditional surrender for purposes of annihilation. It has implicit in it a tremendous pride: we are the people; wisdom was born with us, and, if we are not careful, may die with us.

Accordingly, while compelled by its own research to grant that the home and the community are essential to the mental health of the whole man, the home, community and church are reduced to a non-cultural level in every intellectual way possible, being limited to a basically emotional influence and none other. In all matters of mind, the initiative must lie with education and the 'scientific' thinker. Such an approach is destructive, however, of every cultural agency, including the home. Again, culture is never the product of the clean-tablet mind or of mind in isolation, but of the whole man, who has now been rendered schizophrenic and sterile by this educational concept.

The erosion of the cultural agencies was furthered by the concept of evolution. In terms of very popular and influential developments of this concept, the family, religion, and all smaller societal forms were relatively primitive forms in human evolution, the culminating form of man's organized life being the cosmopolitan and ultimately world state. The more primitive forms of organization had to be self-consciously outgrown; at best, they were to survive as subsidiary agencies of the State. Consider, for example, the opinion, very influential in its day, of Ch. Letourneau, general secretary to the Anthropological Society of Paris and professor of anthropology:

But this new collectivity will in no way be copied from the primitive clan. Whether it be called State, district, canton, or commune, its government will at once be despotic and liberal; it will repress everything that would be calculated to injure the community, but in everything else it will endeavor to leave the most complete independence to individuals. Our actual family circle is most often imperfect: so few families can give, or know how to give, a healthy physical, moral, and intellectual education to the child, that in this domain large encroachments of the State, whether small or great, are probable, even desirable. There is, in fact, a great social interest before which the pretended rights of families must be effaced. In order to prosper and live, it is necessary that the ethnic or social unit should incessantly produce a sufficient number of individuals well endowed in body, heart, and mind. Before this primordial need all prejudices must yield, all egoistic interests must bend.

But the family and marriage are closely connected; the former cannot be modified so long as the latter remains unchanged. If the legal ties of the family are stretched, while social ties are drawn closer, marriage will have the same fortune. For a long time, more or less silently, a slow work of disintegration has begun, and we see it accentuated every day.[4]

Such thinking was very far from extreme. Indeed, one of the amazing facts of modern times is that the corrosive effects of evolutionary thinking on modern culture, deadly as they have been, have not been totally destructive of freedom and culture. The evolutionary concept became the vehicle of every form of cultural hostility and antinomianism.[5]

As has been indicated, of late the home and other community groups have received a measure of rehabilitation in educational circles, but only in that they are essential to the emotional health of the individual. They cannot presume to extend their scope beyond that. Man as thinker must be cosmopolitan. His true home

[4] Ch. Letourneau: *The Evolution of Marriage*, p. 356. The Contemporary Science Series. London: The Walter Scott Publ. Co., 1911. Third Edition.
[5] See Richard Hofstadter: *Social Darwinsim in American Thought*. Boston: Beacon Press, 1955.

must be the one-world, and his family, humanity. Lesser loyalties are unhealthy and sickly loyalties if they are not outgrown.

Another important aspect of this clean tablet concept of education is that it is destructive of the very idea of education, in that it is reduced to *conditioning*. The mind is regarded as essentially passive, and hence best educated in terms of conditioning. Pavlov's experiment with the conditioning of dogs has not been fully accepted by contemporary educators, of course, but Pavlov shared in common with educators certain concepts concerning the mind as essentially passive and susceptible to conditioning. The word educate, derived from the Latin, *e,* out, *duco,* lead, means to bring out abilities and talents in the person and thus to develop him in terms of himself. This too is the biblical concept in part. As Keil and Delitzsch translated Proverbs 22:6, "Give to the child instruction conformably to his way; So he will not, when he becomes old, depart from it." But the clean tablet concept wants to do no such thing; it is not concerned with education but a radical re-creation of the person beyond anything envisaged by any religion. It is a radically messianic and religious program, aiming at the re-creation of man and his total culture.

And yet, precisely because of its schizophrenic nature and its rootlessness, it is unable to create culture. The total contribution of the university, for example, to modern culture is very limited and, in spite of itself, against its own principles. Its greatest single contribution has perhaps been the underlying work behind the atom bomb, a fitting symbol of its educational theory.

By contrast, let us examine briefly one aspect of the education against which the Enlightenment rebelled, Calvinistic or Reformed education as manifested in the Pilgrims and Puritanism, contemporaneously with the Enlightenment. The Puritans were not past-bound, in that they did not look back to any past state, but sought rather to create a new order. They were, however, past-bound from the viewpoint of the Enlightenment in that they held to the infallible word, the once-for-all and full revelation of God, the Bible. They looked to the future but refused to be chained to it. Thus, the communism of the Pilgrims was quickly dropped when it failed. But, most important of all for our concern, education was a major interest, but on radically different presuppositions. New light was yet to break forth from the infallible word. New developments of society in terms of the fundamental faith were to be manifested. Basic to education were two religious concepts, the *covenant* and *confirmation*. Confirmation, a common Christian practice, had stronger roots often in other groups, but the covenant concept was strongest among Calvinists, and far more important in terms of education. The theological aspects of the doctrine of the covenant are not our concern here, although they do have extensive sociological implications. But two aspects of the covenant immediately concern us. The covenant of grace was a covenant of *life* and with *promise*. Man's every hope in terms of fulfillment and enjoyment, in terms of participation in the richness of life and community, was in terms of the covenant. Education was thus inevitably a *covenantal act,* an incorporation of the person into the life of a rich and vital body, an indoctrination into its past and a participation in its present and future life and power. The covenant, however, was not static; it was a covenant with promise, both for this life and the life to come. In terms of this life, for example, it looked to the beating of swords into plowshares, the earth filled with "the knowledge of the LORD, as the waters cover the sea" (Isa. 11:9), and the time when life expectancy will be such that "the child shall die an hundred years old; but the sinner being an hundred years old shall be accursed. And they shall build houses, and inhabit them . . . They shall not labour in vain, nor bring forth for trouble; for they are the seed of the blessed of the LORD, and their offspring with them" (Isa. 65:20,21,23). This was believed to be the promise of an absolute God who cannot lie; it was taught, for example, in the last century at Princeton by the great Joseph Addison Alexander. Covenant theology was a doctrine of salvation, a plan of conduct, and a philosophy of history as well as the foundation of education.[6] Thus education was an inevitable concern, and it was seen, not as a break with the community and a separation of the "intellectual" from the "peasant," but an aspect of the image mandate within the framework of the covenant. Education, as an aspect of the covenantal life, could not see itself as called to foster rootlessness but to implement the covenant's development of its *life* and *promises*. It did not function to sever home ties, for example, but to confirm them, in that it worked to develop more fully man's knowledge, righteousness, holiness and dominion in terms of every aspect of life. It was thus concerned with the development of godly scholarship, and godly youth who would also be godly sons and daughters now and husbands, wives and parents tomorrow. Confirmation was full adoption into the inheritance from the past and the promises of the future. Emancipation was into the forms of culture and life and not from them. Of these, the state was but one. Cosmopolitanism was not an ideal; rather, it was a major sin, in that it involved the offense of the tower of Babel, a commonality in which the covenant of grace was destroyed in favor of an indifference to good and evil, a proscription of character and merit in favor of wickedness and sloth, and a rebellion against the primacy of faith in favor of a meaningless and dangerous unity. It was a concept they opposed religiously, and hence the Westminster Confession did not hesitate, together with the Reformers, to identify the Church of Rome with the Whore of Babylon and the papacy with the Man of Sin. They opposed it also politically, and the lingering elements of Puritanism in the United States today are usually the areas of hostility to internationalism and the United Nations.

Thus, between the two concepts of education, the Calvinistic and that of the Enlightenment and contemporary thought, there

[6] For an analysis of the implications in terms of Christian education in the church, see L. B. Schenck: *The Presbyterian Doctrine of Children in the Covenant*. New Haven: Yale U. Press, 1940. For the implications of the modern concepts in the life of the church, see H. Shelton Smith: *Faith and Nurture*. New York: Scribner, 1941. For an important study of the breakdown of the concept, see Peter Y. De Jong: *The Covenant Idea in New England Theology, 1620-1847*, Grand Rapids: Eerdmans, 1945.

can be no compromise. They are in hopeless contradiction. The modern concept, with its cosmopolitanism and its clean-tablet ideal, is erosive and destructive of all aspects of culture except the monolithic state, which is then the ostensible creator and patron of culture. When it speaks of the whole child, it speaks of a passive creature who is to be molded by statist education for a concept of the good life radically divorced from God and from all transcendental standards. The goal of such education will only be reached when man ceases to be man, and, this being an impossibility, the only outcome of such education can be the increasing resistance of the child to its radical implications.

Modern education thus is statist education, and the state is made the all-embracing institution of which all other institutions are but facets. The state and the person, government and individual, become thus the two realities of such a world-view. Both demand freedom and power for themselves. The state recognizes no law beyond itself and the individual insists on his own autonomy and ultimacy. But the child of the state, being a man without faith, has no vital principle of resistance and thus even in his rebellion is statist. Every philosophy of autonomous man from the Greeks to the present has foundered on the problem of the one and the many, universality and particularity. If the one be affirmed as the ultimate reality, the individuals are swallowed up in the whole. If the many be affirmed, then reality is lost in endless particularity and individuality, and no binding concept has any reality. Thus, the one and the many are in perpetual tension. The individual and the state, for example, can only each affirm themselves at the expense of the other.

Against this, the consistent Christian philosophy, as developed by Calvinistic thinkers such as Kuyper, Bavinck and C. Van Til, by beginning with the biblical revelation and the ontological trinity, begins thereby with the equal ultimacy and the fundamental congeniality of the one and the many in the trinity, three persons, one God. The concept of the covenant furthers this unity in that the self-realization of the individual is the advantage of all and is advanced by and integral with the self-realization of others. In the modern conception, the fulfilment and self-realization of the individual are at the expense of others and may involve their sacrifice. For the orthodox Christian, self-realization apart from the covenant is an impossibility, and it involves life in an organism, the true body of Christ. This latter concept, the body of Christ, asserts emphatically in all its biblical statements that individuality is not monotonous repetition but the fulfilment of varying functions and callings as individuals who are yet part of a common whole. The service of the body requires the fulfilment of the individual; the eye must fulfil itself as an eye that the entire body as well may prosper. Covenantal education is thus education which is not at odds with itself and the nature of man. It has been accused of being no more than "mere indoctrination," but indoctrination is after all no more than teaching in terms of principles and the teaching of principles. Covenantal education is that, and much more. But it is definitely not conditioning, nor can it be, for it holds man to be not a passive and blank object, nor a creature of the state, but God's vicegerent, created in His image and called upon to establish dominion over all creation—and over himself. This calling, with its responsibilities and consequences, no electroshock concept of education can alter or remove.

2

The Purpose of Knowledge

Modern man has been extensively instructed in the sexual life of savages, their social customs, fertility rites and educational practices, with some very real profit to the publishers involved. Whether Western marital life has been edified by the knowledge that passionate Melanesians bite off one another's eye-lashes in the heat of love is possibly open to question.[1] Behind much of the production and consumption of such information stands, however, a highly respectable theory, one which has become an unconscious article of faith: "Knowledge is power."

For Francis Bacon, as he expounded it in his "Aphorisms Concerning the Interpretation of Nature and the Kingdom of Man" in *Novum Organum,* man is "the servant and interpreter of nature" rather than of God. This is in radical departure from the biblical concept of Psalm 8, affirming man to be king over creation under God. Again, in Aphorism III, Bacon asserted,

Human knowledge and human power meet in one; for where the cause is not known the effect cannot be produced. Nature

[1] Bronislaw Malinowski: *The Sexual Life of Savages,* p. 297. New York: Halcyon House, 1929.

12

to be commanded must be obeyed; and that which in contemplation is as the cause is in operation as the rule.

Among other things the scientific approach for Bacon was characterized by the requirement for an exhaustive collection of particulars in each scientific inquiry (an insuperable requirement, never met), and the requirement that the scientist recognize no fact or conclusion until it first passes muster under the test of his particular methodology, unless the scientist, to use Bacon's expression, act like the spider spinning a web out of himself rather than like an ant which merely collects materials.

The consequences of this position have been far-reaching. Moral inertia and cowardice are no new things in history, but they function now on two new grounds. Men hesitate to act on the sufficient knowledge that they have, because it is not exhaustive, as though such knowledge were possible. Again, men collect knowledge of evil as though the public proclamation of the facts gave some power over evil.

Bacon's aphorism was in a limited sense true; nature, to be controlled, has to be known. But the knowledge in itself does not effect the control.

The modern attitude, which looks to science for so many social values, has made an ugly fact out of "investigation." More than one political reputation has been made on the basis of investigations and hearings, as witness Kefauver, with the main consequences being that at least one hapless witness died for telling the truth. Many a business man, worker, or police officer, under the wretched illusion that some current investigation offered hope of reform, has testified to his or her ruin. A double fallacy is involved in these hearings: 1. The moral fallacy—if only they hear the truth, people will demand a reform. But hardly a single investigation has taken place in recent years which did not already cover familiar ground. The public interest is usually not in the truth or reform but in the pleasures of scandal. 2. The educational fallacy, that knowledge is power, that the proclamation of the facts of evil, for example, is tantamount to the control of evil.

As a result, investigations have come to play a major role in the modern era. They have been frequently a substitute for action, and, worse yet, in the hands of some men, have been used to smear worthy men and causes. The Industrial Revolution is still viewed by most people, including scholars, through the smear investigations, with their partial truths, of aristocrats who resented the rise of the entrepreneurs.[2]

From the Christian point of view, failure to act on knowledge is a sin. From the modern point of view, "find the facts" makes sense but there is often impotence with regard to action on the facts. This impotence is often heightened by the reserved judgment required by the scientific ideal of exhaustive knowledge. To refer, without the details, to the conclusions of a minor investigation which revealed the dishonesty of a particular official, it is revealing to note the reasons for failure to act, after long and somewhat costly investigation. First, "You never know all the facts," although the fact of dishonesty and misappropriation was known. Second, "What does guilty mean, anyway?" Besides, restitution of *known* losses was being made, and all was smoothed over. This incident, too minor to attract more than a passing local interest, is important nonetheless. *Without a true concept of responsibility, it is hard to have a crime, or, for that matter, any virtue.* Today it is a question in many minds *if* or *when* any person is responsible. His heredity, environment, parental background have all conditioned him; instead of punishment, he needs reconditioning in order that the desired results may follow. Punishment, which assumes guilt and responsibility, is barbaric, capital punishment most of all. Suddeny we find that *knowledge has abdicated to conditioning as the means of power!*

The scientific ideal of knowledge has another facet which has been heavily influential in modern thought. Scientifically, a hypothesis is usable if it is the theory which does justice to the most

[2] See Ludwig Von Mises: *Human Action*, A Treatise on Economics, pp. 613-19, New Haven: Yale U. Press, 1949. See also W. H. Hutt, "The Factory System of the Early Nineteenth Century," pp. 160-188 in F. A. Hayek, ed., *Capitalism and the Historians*, Chicago, U. of Chicago Press, 1954.

facts. It is a kind of common denominator for a particular group of facts. In science, such a procedure may have its validity, but is it applicable elsewhere? It has been very generally applied, in ethics, religion, the "social sciences" and elsewhere. In ethics, it began by collecting, long ago, parallel passages to the Golden Rule, all wrenched out of context, and reading a common meaning into very diverse declarations. A contemporary group uses the Sermon on the Mount similarly, declaring, in large newspaper advertisements, "In an important sense, we feel this sermon represents the strife and distilled wisdom of all the prophets of all time: Akhenaten, Moses, Zoroaster, Jeremiah, Confucius, Buddha, Jesus, Mohammed; and others unrecorded thruout centuries before any of these. All along, their essential teachings have surely pointed the way to sane conduct, within the universal discipline and challenge of 'God.' " Apart from the radical historical violence of this statement, and its confident inclusion of unknown and unrecorded "prophets," the significant fact is that God appears with "quotes," and properly so. He is, after all, only the common denominator of all men's ideas, and the ultimate source of truth and revelation is the mass concurrence of men. Only thus can true value appear. Some have derived "true" or "natural" religion by this methodology. The end result of such an approach is to be found in Kinsey, who could list and equate animal contacts and homosexuality with heterosexuality as alike natural and hence normal.[3] In this concept, knowledge becomes equivalent to permissiveness rather than power, and the psychiatric data indicates that permissiveness leads to impotence rather than power. *Knowledge as statistical incidence* never leads to power; it only witnesses to the cultural predilection and preference for a certain form of behavior. But knowledge as statistical incidence is still a compelling force socially.

However, with the waning faith in democracy, Marxism, and the masses, the conception of knowledge as statistical incidence

[3] See Edmund Bergler and William S. Kroger: *Kinsey's Myth of Female Sexuality*, New York, Grune and Stratton, 1954.

has in some quarters given way to a more Freudian concept. The orthodox Christian doctrine of the infallible word of God, the Bible, as the ground of all true knowledge and itself inerrant, has its secular analogue in the Freudian doctrine of the infallibility and inerrancy of the subsconscious. Freud assumed the validity of every aspect of this new word. Here was an area of self-revelation where no "error" was possible. The very concept of the "Freudian slip" assumes that even the most casual mistake of speech is a part of this new infallible word forcing itself through the sick facade of the consciousness. There was much of Rousseau in Freud, although a much less optimistic trust in nature. No evidence for this infallibility concept has been given, nor can any significant addition to knowledge be ascribed to it. There is perhaps some comfort in this fact, because it would be a little trying to live easily with all that awesome infallibility under one's skin!

At any rate, man has become less and less sure what constitutes knowledge, and, in identifying both knowledge and value with statistical incidence, has destroyed both. As Weaver has pointed out, "values begin divisions among men."[4] Values are fundamentally divisive. But man is hostile too often to "divisive" values, and so the values he prizes are in effect anti-values, attempts to reduce religion, ethics, or whatever value he seeks, to an all-inclusive level. For example it is said that a loving God cannot permit the existence of hell; therefore, everyone must go to heaven. Since heaven must include Jack the Ripper and Hitler under these circumstances, this loving God must re-condition them for their new existence. Violence is thus done to values wholesale, and to the integrity of God, heaven, and man.

This problem is important, because man's concept of knowledge is oriented to his concept of values. What the Indian medicine man considered true knowledge is hardly the scientists' definition of it, and the difference is in their basic philosophy and

[4] Richard M. Weaver, *Ideas Have Consequences* (Chicago: U. of Chicago Press, 1948) p. 59.

values. The scientist was not born full-grown from the head of Zeus; he is a cultural product, having basic to his science certain assumptions which are the product of Hellenic, Christian, medieval, and modern humanist influences. Now, however, the old certainties are open to doubt, and the values often more personal than social. Indeed, values are regarded increasingly as an area of personal free choice rather than social necessity.

The consequence has been the development of an odd filing cabinet concept of mind and man. All framework of reference being gone, man has for the most part one filing classification left: miscellaneous. The "group" in progressive education is only a larger miscellaneous item than the individual. Man's knowledge today is Alexandrian, masses of detail without a focus. But man cannot give to his knowledge a focus which he himself does not possess.

Consider the focus which man increasingly manifests. Riesman, Glazer and Denney have called attention to the fact that man has become consumption-centered rather than production-centered, has made the group the source of morality and the framework of reference, has made in some instances understanding a substitute for power, has become other-directed rather than inner-directed and shifted the emphasis from morality to morale, and has enthroned the feelings of the group into a position of deity.[5] All of this is well illustrated in the December 28, 1959 double issue of *Life* magazine, entitled "The Good Life." About two hundred extravagant pages are given to defining "the good life" in terms of two things, play and "love, the elixer." Nothing is said about God, in relation to whom the good life was once defined, nor about work and learning. Here, without question, is a child's conception of the good life, love and play, but that child is increasingly modern man everywhere. As it has been observed, man once lived to work, but now he works to live, i.e., to play.

---

[5] See David Riesman, Nathan Glazer, Reuel Denney: *The Lonely Crowd, A Study of the Changing American Character*, Garden City, N.Y. Doubleday Anchor Bks., 1953.

The same is true of knowledge. Man's goal in knowledge is increasingly release from the responsibility of knowledge. Curriculum changes are often urgently needed, but, in the face of this studied infantilism, not enough.

Long before Bacon, man set himself a false ideal for knowledge. Man's original sin involved the postulate of an ultimate epistemological and metaphysical pluralism which gave equal ultimacy to the mind of man and of God, as well as to time and eternity. Hence, there was no eternal decree, and only time could be the test of anything, together with experimentation and exhaustive knowledge. In terms of this, true knowledge became either illusory or at very best tentative.

Against this, the orthodox Christian doctrine asserts that man was created in the image of God, which means not only that he was created in knowledge, righteousness, holiness, and dominion, but, more broadly, that no aspect of man's life and experience exists apart from the mediation of that image. Man, though fallen, is still inescapably tied, in all his experience, to the reality and the knowledge of his origin. Man was called to exercise his knowledge and dominion over the created universe as vicegerent under God and to His glory. And, according to Proverbs 1:7, "the fear of the Lord is the beginning (or, chief part, R.V.mg.) of knowledge." In other words, knowledge is no mere collection of data; it is data seen in relationship to God as the sovereign and almighty one. Knowledge comes from God; it is the reverential subordination of all knowing to the Creator. Man cannot identify himself in terms of himself, nor, ultimately, can he sustain any knowledge in terms of himself. Autonomous man must know everything or he knows nothing if he be consistent to his principle. This ideal of exhaustive knowledge claims far more than the biblical revelation, which definitely does not assert itself to be exhaustive. The biblical revelation, however, definitely undergirds all reality. As Van Til has observed, "The best, the only, the absolutely certain proof of the truth of Christianity is that unless its truth be presupposed there is no proof of anything.

Christianity is proved as being the very foundation of the idea of proof itself."[6]

Knowledge, separated from the basic premise, tends to disintegrate, and to be prostituted. More than that, the concept of the man of knowledge, the scholar, also disintegrates. The Reformation began as a movement of Christian scholarship, and for some time the centrality of the scholar persisted.[7] Scholarship, which, under Luther, gained so exalted a place in the German nation, disappeared in its integrity and respect when true Lutheran faith waned also.[8] The high calling of Christian priesthood was involved in scholarship, but the priesthood waned as the faith behind it waned. The rise of pietism within the church made experience, as in Romanticism, central, and scholarship came to be despised.

Scholars have often been used and honored by various cultures, but in an unhappy sense, in that, however much they may be respected and followed, they are not regarded as normal or true men. In one sense, Oriental culture is a significant exception to this; in another, the Oriental scholar, having adopted a radical relativism and abandoned the concept of truth, was merely a learned source of social cement and a learned obstacle to true scholarship. In other cultures, however, the scholar has in varying degrees had something of the character of the Eskimo shaman, whose calling requires a developed, controlled and accepted schizophrenia in the clinical sense.[9] With the Eskimos, we have a clinically mature case of schizophrenia socially required of the shaman. Other cultures have analogous requirements of medicine men, priests, etc. While there are marked differences, and the analogy cannot be forced too far, modern culture does have

[6] Cornelius Van Til: *A Christian Theory of Knowledge* p. 224. 1954.

[7] See E. Harris Harbison: *The Christian Scholar in the Age of the Reformation*, New York, Scribner, 1956.

[8] Eugen Rosenstock-Huessy: *Out of Revolution*, pp. 366-442, New York, William Morrow, 1938.

[9] Margaret Lantis, "The Religion of the Eskimo." p. 316 f. in Vergilius Ferm, ed. *Ancient Religions*. A Symposium. New York: Philosophical Library, 1950.

similarly schizophrenic conceptions and expectations of the man of knowledge. An age concerned with its own consumption and play is bound to think of the pursuit of knowledge as divisive to the human soul and as something not quite normal. Thus the scientist appears both as an immaculate, pure and selfless nun in a holy quest and a mad monster seeking to destroy the world. The artist is coarse, sensual and crude, and yet too much above earthly matters to be concerned with business details. The professor is an absent-minded bumbler and yet at the same time a dangerous man who is trying to undermine society. Scholarship and learning are not the life of "normal" man and they are assumed to exact a schizophrenic penalty of all devotees.

And yet the biblical concept of man's vocation and prophetic role requires us to believe that the true scholar is the normal man, and any other attitude is sub-Christian. Modern man is eccentric in the literal meaning of that word, off center. Apart from true faith, his life is off center. His culture, at its very best, and leavened extensively by Christian presuppositions, is still guilty of eccentricity. He forces eccentricity on every aspect of his society, and on his modern shaman, the scientist. "The Good Life," play and "love the elixir," he reserves unto himself with the unhappy infantilism of senility.

Against all this the Christian scholar must protest. Scholarship is a prophetic, priestly, and kingly function, a central part of man's creation mandate. The godly scholar is the true man, and the school an essential part of the Kingdom of God.

3

The Unity of Learning

Heretofore, every culture has had its means of educating its young into the meaning of their heritage. The learning of and initiation into the life of that society has not been a question of coercion but a means of life. As a result, education has not been a problem but an assumed part of life, essential to maturity, to the assumption of their destined roles of man or woman, farmer, hunter, or warrior. This, of course, is no longer true, Society has reached a degree of security and self-consciousness which has separated culture from life and made it, on the one hand, a self-conscious striving after superiority, status, or higher values, and, on the other, a reduction of culture to protected and indulged folk feelings which imply a contempt of those who seek "advance."

Again, society has ceased to be society and has become pluralistic and atomistic. A man has no common life with most of society and seeks a limited circle as his arena of activity, an arena in terms of which, rather than in terms of the total society and its faith, he seeks status.

It has been said that our's is a pluralistic society because of its very progress, and pluralism is essential to our development out of the unity of folk culture, and, in a sense, we can most definitely agree with this. There is, however, a difference between an atomistic culture and a pluralistic one. The one has a variety of competing meanings, each with its inner unity and integrity, whereas the other is the collapse of society into its fragmentary elements. Ostensibly, Western culture, having its varying representatives of Christian churches, humanism in a variety of forms, and other cultural divisions, is pluralistic. But the pluralism is nominal, external and extrinsic. Actually an atomistic society is one reduced to certain common denominators which fail to sustain any single element. The possibility of deep-rooted tensions tends to be reduced, because meaning is reduced. The tensions which are generated are in terms of *power* and *control* rather than *meaning*. This is no less true of communists today than any other group; their concern is not the spread of world socialism but the control of the world by their particular form of it. Churches are likewise less concerned over *doctrine* and more over *power*.

What, in brief, is this current common denominator? Christianity has by and large been debased into vague and sentimental love of man, a reduction of God into love alone, and an anarchistic conception of the requirements of love. No more telling instance of this can be cited than the widely acclaimed and extensively used *Basic Christian Ethics* of Paul Ramsey (1950), associate professor of Religion at Princeton University. This same element, in other forms, appears in the Church of Rome, of which Francis of Assisi was an early representative. With this also goes divinizing strains. Notice the implications of the following statements by the editor of a current edition of an old ascetic manual: "Deification is the ultimate fulfilling of human nature's capacity for God . . . deification and salvation are the same."[1] Humanism has become a vague belief in man and in

[1] St. Maximus the Confessor: *The Ascetic Life, The Four Centuries on Charity*, p. 71. Translated and annotated by Polycarp Sherwood. Westminster, Md., The Newman Press, 1955.

"values" but becomes progressively more incapable of defining values, and, in existentialism, is in full-fledged retreat from life.

According, if we are to understand the concept of the unity of learning from the biblical perspective, we must re-examine it in terms of its basic concepts, ones largely by-passed in the current anarchistic and sentimentalized forms of Christianity.

The biblical principles of the unity of learning must inevitably be drawn from Scripture itself. To import alien principles is to destroy any possibility of comprehension and to force Scripture into an alien mold. Basic to our interest, therefore is a careful understanding of the biblical doctrine of revelation and wisdom. Very early, we find the fundamental unity of "the word" asserted, Israel being forbidden to add or diminish from "the word" (Deut. 4:2). "Words" could be added, until the end (Rev. 22:18 f.), but not another "word." Again, we are repeatedly told that "Wisdom" is the source of "the word," and in Proverbs we are given a concept of wisdom whereby wisdom is closely associated with the Godhead.

Let us examine, very briefly, some of the statements of Proverbs 8 alone:

1. The world was created by Wisdom, and Wisdom was the principle of its creation, vv. 22-31.
2. Man was a part of Wisdom's plan of creation; "and my delight was with the sons of men," v. 31.
3. Wisdom summons man to live in terms of Wisdom and in righteousness, vv. 1-12, 32-36.
4. Wisdom mediates between God and man, vv. 32-35.
5. The love of Wisdom is the love of life, "But he that sinneth against me wrongeth his own soul: All they that hate me love death," v. 36.
6. Wisdom is the ground of all law and order, of all peace and prosperity, of life itself, vv. 13-21.

Turning now to the New Testament, we find the same concept of Wisdom set forth:

1. Jesus Christ declared himself to be Wisdom, Luke 7:34, 35; Matt. 11:19.
2. Jesus Christ is declared to be the Word, Logos, or Wisdom of God, John 1:1-17.
3. He spoke of his pre-existence, John 8:58.
4. Paul also declared him to be the Logos or Wisdom of God, I Cor. 1:24,30; Comp. Rom. 13:27, Col. 2:3.

Returning again to Proverbs 8:15, we find this important declaration, "By me kings reign, and princes decree justice." In forcing their presuppositions on Scripture, men have reversed the meaning of this statement, assuming it merely to be the ordination of secular government; in actuality far more is involved here. "By me kings reign, and princes decree justice," means that the very ground of justice is Wisdom itself, that, apart from Wisdom, there is no decree of justice, no law nor order, that the ground of all life, of all law and order, of all structure, all design in creation, comes from God. This same principle is developed by Paul in Ephesians, where we have an amazingly far-reaching declaration of the meaning of the glorified Christ for all of life. In that context, in Eph. 3:15, Paul speaks of God as the father of all families, or, more literally, the father of all fatherhoods. Later, in Eph. 5:22-33, he speaks of the marital relationship of husband and wife as a type of Christ and the church. Now the usual humanistic approach to these statements is a reversal of the order of precedence and says in effect, "Paul, trying to make these divine mysteries plain, took ordinary human standards and facts, and stated that these things, very dimly, vaguely, represent to us the divine mysteries which cannot be known. Thus, the reality is the family, the father and his children which in a faint way, gives us the divine reality behind it. This is anthropomorphic speech." Actually, the reverse is true. It is not the human family, the human fatherhood, which is the basic reality; rather, for Paul it is the type or shadow, and the fatherhood of God is the ultimate reality. The relationship of Christ to His church is the basic reality of which the relationship of husband to wife is a shadow, a setting forth of the same principle. God is the father of all fatherhoods, and human fatherhood is but a faint reflection of the eternal relationship of the ontological trinity, of the Father to the Son. Our human fellowship, governments, relationships, are shadows therefore of a reality which exists in the internal relationship of the Father, the Son, and the Holy Ghost. All the basic relationships of life therefore are derived from the eternal standard of the internal life of the Godhead. Here then is the basic biblical premise which the concept of anthropomorphisms by-passes and destroys. In terms of this concept of Wisdom, the priority in all categories of thought of the ontological trinity, there is no law, no society, no justice, no structure, no design, no meaning apart from God and all these aspects and relationships of society are types of that which exists in the Godhead.

This, accordingly, has a tremendous implication in terms of the unity of life and learning. Wherever man asserts his independence of God, saying in effect, that, while he will deny God, he will not deny life, nor its relationships, values, or society, its science and art, he is involved in contradiction. In terms of these neglected biblical presuppositions, it is an impossibility for man to deny God and still to have law and order, justice, science, anything, apart from God. The more man and society depart from God, the more they depart from all reality, the more they are caught in the net of self-contradiction and self-frustration, the more they are involved in the will to destruction and the love of death (Prov. 8:36). "By me kings reign, and princes decree justice." "All they that hate me love death." For man to turn his back on God, therefore, is to turn towards death; it involves ultimately the renunciation of every aspect of life. Thus, every government, whether it be a Christian state or not, cannot live apart from God. In so far as it has any kind of law and order, any kind of justice, it is a traitor to itself, because it thereby affirms God. Likewise, every science, however it may outwardly deny God, if it asserts that there is fundamental structure and law in the universe, as exemplified for instance in the Second

Law of Thermodynamics, is a traitor to itself, because while denying God, it works in terms of fundamental structures which are an impossibility apart from God.

To deny God, man must ultimately deny that there is any law, or reality. The full implications of this were seen in the last century by two profound thinkers, one a Christian, the other a non-Christian. Nietzsche recognized fully that every atheist is an unwilling believer to the extent that he has any element of justice or order in his life, to the very extent that he is even alive and enjoys life. In his earlier writings, Nietzsche first attempted the creation of another set of standards and values, affirming life for a time, until he concluded that he could not affirm life itself, nor give it any meaning, any value, apart from God. Thus Nietzsche's ultimate counsel was suicide; only then, can we truly deny God, and, in his own life, this brilliant thinker, one of the clearest in his description of modern Christianity and the contemporary issue, did in effect commit a kind of psychic suicide.[2] The same concept was powerfully developed by Dostoyevsky, particularly in *The Possessed,* or, more literally, the Demon Possessed. Kirilov, a thoroughly Nietzschean character, is very much concerned with denying God, asserting that he himself is God, and that man does not need God. But at every point, Kirilov finds that no standard or structure in reality can be affirmed without ultimately asserting God, that no value can be asserted without being ultimately derived from the triune God. As a result, Kirilov committed suicide as the only apparently practical way of denying God and affirming himself, for to be alive was to affirm this ontological deity in some fashion.

The philosophical implications of all this have been lost on the wretched and beggarly thinking which has characterized so much of Christian philosophy. Happily, in recent years there has been a development of a consistent Christian philosophy, beginning with Abraham Kuyper's use of Calvin's premise, and ad-

[2] For an exceptionally brilliant analysis of Nietzsche from this perspective, see H. Van Riessen: *Nietzsche*. Philadelphia: Presbyterian and Reformed, 1960.

vanced powerfully in this country by Cornelius Van Til. This position is that affirmed in all of Scripture. Consider the implications of the following passages:

1. Wisdom in Prov. 3:18 is called the tree of life.
2. In John 8:51, "If any man keep my sayings, he shall never see death."
3. "Evil men understand not judgment, but they that seek the Lord understand all things," Prov. 28:5.
4. Again, in I John 2:20, we have this far-reaching statement, "But ye have an unction from the Holy One, and ye know all things."

These are amazing affirmations: "They that seek the Lord understand all things." "Ye have an unction from the Holy One, and ye know all things." Clearly, our knowledge of all things is not exhaustive or particular, nor is our knowledge omniscient; such knowledge is possible only with God. How then do we actually know all things? Let us re-examine this statement: if, when we become truly Christian and are aware of its true implications, having the unction of the Holy One, we know all things, conversely, if we have not Christ, an unction from the Holy One, we know nothing. Thus we must say to the unbeliever, "For all your learning, you know nothing." On the other hand, a consistently Christian education, having this concept of the unity of learning, must affirm, to be a Christian, and have an unction from the Holy One, means to know all things in principle. This means that, in knowing Christ, we know Him by whom all things were made, and without Him was not anything made that was made (John 1:1-17). As a result, nothing is understandable except in terms of Christ, in terms of his creative will. All secular learning is involved in a fundamental contradiction: it must act on the assumption of a unity of law and meaning while denying the very existence of it or its implications. It acts on the premise of the sovereignty of law while it asserts chance. "By Him were all things made, and without him was not anything made that was made." No interpretation or meaning can *logically* exist apart from Him.

There is an eternal decree, an eternal purpose, and nothing is understandable except in terms of that presupposition. Knowing Christ we know all things; we have the fundamental principle of interpretation. Secular learning is involved in self-contradiction, is continually denying itself. For example, in the study of the theory of numbers in so many universities, when dealing with the question of what a number is, it is denied that a number has any correspondence with reality. But if numbers have no correspondence to reality, why study mathematics? If arithmetic and mathematics have no relationship to life, if they are simply arbitrary, why study them? But to affirm a relationship to reality, a fundamental reality represented in numbers, is to affirm that there is a fundamental reality to which man is accountable. In the study of philosophy and the theory of values, we again face this same relativity. Education then becomes much ado about nothing. Why the concern for advances in education when all is set in the context of present and ultimate relativity? Why this tremendous energy to create values in education and in society if relativity governs all? Why laws? Nietzsche was here more honest than Dewey. There are philosophers who have felt it essential to all philosophies of science that they deny the concept of causality, for to assert causality is in some fashion to assert an eternal decree behind all reality. Hence, in the place of causality, the concept of probability is affirmed, which says in effect that thus far we have found phenomena dependable, but we have no way of knowing that, in the next instance, a completely contrary phenomenon may not appear. By this bit of dodging, the implications of causality are side-stepped. To assert causality is to assert ultimately and by implication an eternal decree behind the phenomena of creation.

Is it any wonder that education is no longer a means of life but a matter of state coercion? In every area we have what can only be characterized as intellectual schizophrenia, a split personality. On the one hand modern man, "Christian" and non-Christian, in dealing with the practical necessities of any particular area of

science or of learning, must be theistic, must assume the ontological trinity, in that he must posit an eternal decree, a unity in life
and learning and a correspondence to ultimate reality of numbers,
etc. Let him *hold* to as radical a relativism as he may, he still
acts in terms of an eternal decree. As a result, he is caught in the
tension of intellectual schizophrenia and is a divided person, a
house divided against itself. The growing tension of modern life
is due precisely to this schizophrenic element in all learning. The
more relevant science and learning become to everyday life, the
more irrelevant they become in theory. Man is schizoid in his
attempt to function apart from God, to use the things of this
creation while denying their creator and the eternal decree behind
all reality. Man apart from God is guilty of what Van Til calls
the Cainitic wish, the desire that there be no God, but whenever
and wherever man tries to eliminate God, he ends up by eliminat-
ing all reality. He has increasingly to deny aspects of his experience and of reality, because no place can be given it in his philosophy. Note, for example, psychologies which refuse to speak of
the mind, and refer in passing to consciousness as an "epiphenom-
enon" outside the scope of relevance. To face consistently the
problem of mind and consciousness is as one writer warned, to
lead to the supernatural. Instead, the language has been one of
drives, impulses, motivations, not of the mind or consciousness.
To eliminate God as the ontological principle is to emasculate
reality. This is seen as clearly in contemporary theology as any-
where, as witness Karl Barth. Barth posits a Kantian God who
is in essence an aspect of human consciousness, is so afraid of
power and being in itself that he maintains that if God were power
in Himself, omnipotent, He would be the devil "For 'the Almighty'
is bad, as 'power in itself' is bad. The 'Almighty' means Chaos,
Evil, the Devil. We could not better describe and define the Devil
than by trying to think this idea of a self-based, free, sovereign
ability."[3] As a consequence, such a philosophy tends to a distrust

[3] Karl Barth: *Dogmatics in Outline*, p. 48. New York: Philosophical Library,
1949.

of all power and dominion, and, in effect, renounces the very creation image-mandate of man, to exercise dominion, to become an appointed bearer of God's power and His vicegerent, and to exercise that dominion in its fullest scope in every area of knowledge. Thus a consistently Christian philosophy of education alone can deal honestly with reality, for, in affirming the Creator, it alone can do justice to creation. By recognizing that God is He by whom all things were made, and without him was not anything made that was made, it affirms the one principle by which we truly can know all things. According to Romans 1:18, as John Murray and others render it, "The wrath of God is revealed from heaven against all ungodliness and unrighteousness of men who *hold down* the truth in unrighteousness." Here is the essence of the matter: truth is inescapable; what characterizes man is not so much a failure in learning as an ethical revolt against the implications of what he knows. He recognizes the eternal decree, sees it everywhere manifested, but holds down the implications of this truth in unrighteousness, and suppresses it because it destroys his autonomy. The result is an insuperable tension. Modern man, being a split personality, schizophrenic, ultimately reaches the crisis, the breakdown of all schizophrenic personalities, in his inability to maintain an existence in such sharp contradiction to itself. Modern education is schizophrenic, holding down the truth as the only means of perpetuating modern man's claim to autonomy. If necessary, all meaning must be denied in order to maintain this strange freedom. A telling instance of this is Herbert J. Muller's comments on "The Misuses of the Past."[4] Muller finds man's freedom precisely in the absence of any governing principle in history and the absence of objective reality apart from man.

To restate the basic biblical premise in order to develop it further, reality is ultimately personal because the ontological trinity is personal. Every aspect of life, society, authority, fatherhood, community, etc., is a shadow or type of the ultimate and

[4] *Horizon*, I, 4, March, 1959.

full reality of the internal relationships of the ontological trinity. Greek philosophy, believing as it did in ultimate impersonalism, developed the concept of anthropomorphism, an idea in terms of which the church has almost consistently and insistently read the Bible. For example, it became important to insist that God is passionless, passion being a frailty of personality, and to read the biblical statements of God's wrath, jealousy, laughter, and delight as anthropomorphisms used in condescension to a primitive humanity.[5] The unhappy consequences of Hellenic thought have been ably traced by Charles Norris Cochrane, *Christianity and Classical Culture* (1940). With Cochrane, we can speak of the classical-modern position as against the Christian. In the classical-modern view, change is ultimate, set in a sea of impersonality. Whatever universals may be affirmed, the good, the true, and the beautiful, remain abstractions, impersonal in essence. The problem of the one and the many becomes insuperable: either a meaningless sea of oneness, or an equally meaningless universe of endless and unrelated particularity. The Christian, on the other hand, working on the premise of the ontological trinity, can think and act on the presupposition of the cotermineity of the universal and the particular in the Godhead. He denies, moreover, the existence of brute factuality; every fact is an interpreted fact. Man either creates his factuality by his own principle of interpretation, and thus becomes his own god, or he accepts the fact of creation and that God's creative purpose alone makes the fact what it is, and that no true interpretation is possible apart from Him. But, as Van Til has observed,

> The idea of brute, that is utterly uninterpreted, "fact" is the presupposition to the finding of any fact of scientific standing. A "fact" does not become a fact according to the modern scientist's assumptions, till it has been made a fact by the ultimate

[5] The Bible is anthropomorphic in the sense that much which is beyond the scope of man's present experience, or beyond the limitations of the creature, is made understandable in such terms. Our point is that to ascribe the idea of God's Fatherhood and other like concepts, to anthropomorphism is to destroy a central aspect of Scripture and prepare the way for impersonalism.

definitory power of the mind of man. The modern scientist, pretending merely to be a describer of facts, is in reality a maker of facts. He makes facts as he describes. His description is itself the manufacturing of facts. He requires "material" to make facts, but the material he requires must be *raw* material. Anything else will break his machinery. The datum is not primarily *given,* but is primarily *taken.*

It appears then that a universal judgment about the nature of all existence is presupposed even in the "description" of the modern scientist. It appears further that this universal judgment negates the heart of the Christian-theistic point of view. According to any consistently Christian position, God, and God only, has ultimate definitory power. God's description or plan of the fact makes the fact what it is. What modern scientist ascribes to the mind of man Christianity ascribes to God.[6]

To consider again the underlying impersonalism of the classical-modern position, its inevitable corollary is this, that *the higher the development of intelligence and culture, the greater its impersonalism, the more necessary its abstractness.* Some religions and philosophies see the goal as the end of the principle of individuation, as absorption into the cosmic sea of nothingness or god, as the case may be. But, man being a person, and his life a very personal matter, it is impossible for a culture to develop this concept of impersonalism without again manifesting a schizoid life. Consider, for example, the consequences in music. At about the same time that music became on the one hand atonal, intellectual, and impersonal, jazz arose at the other end of the musical scale to affirm an anti-intellectual and completely atomistic personalism. One of the defenders of jazz has stated, "Jazz has no need of intelligence; it needs only feeling."[7]

---

[6] C. Van Til: *Common Grace,* p. 4 (1947). See also Van Til's *The New Modernism* (1946). *The Defense of the Faith* (1955), *The Metaphysics of Apologetics* (1931), *A Christian Theory of Knowledge* (1954), etc, and R. J. Rushdoony, *By What Standard?* 1959, all published by Presbyterian and Reformed Pub. Co.

[7] Cited from Robert Goffin, *Jazz,* p. 42, by Richard M. Weaver, *Ideas Have Consequences,* p. 85.

Both extremes represent triumphs of musical virtuosity, certainly, but, more than that, both exist in terms of an assumed ultimacy of impersonalism. This impersonality "intellectual" music celebrates at the price of its wider appeal. This impersonality jazz reacts against with a wild and hopeless personalism, with an eat, drink and be merry, for tomorrow we die, philosophy. It is, as Weaver has remarked "a music not of dreams—certainly not of our metaphysical dream—but of drunkenness."[8] And yet the strength of jazz is precisely its presentation of an available personalism in a world of impersonalism, and hence its appeal in Communist countries, where so much more rigorous an impersonalism of life and philosophy prevails. So powerful is the impact of jazz on the Communist peoples, that some jazz musicians have come to fancy themselves as symbols of freedom, which, in an extremely limited sense, they are. And yet the blind affirmation of an anarchistic emotionalism is no weapon against the tyranny of impersonalism, whether of the universe, society, or mass man, but a tribute to its power and a surrender of the rest of life to impersonalism. In art, a similar picture appears, a coincidence in the rise of abstractionism and a totally personal and incommunicative emotionalism. In poetry, a similar development has occurred; a poem need no longer "mean" something but must only "be."

The details can be cited at length. Suffice it to say that they merely repeat this fact: when impersonalism is assumed to be ultimate, then the higher the development of intelligence and culture, the greater its impersonalism, the more necessary its abstractness. Because man cannot accept this necessary conclusion to his cultural striving, he himself being too personal a fact, he inevitably becomes schizophrenic in his life and culture. His education accordingly loses all concept of any unity of learning. Progressive education has tried to remedy this lack and give relationship to learning by relating it to everyday life. But the relationship is made at the wrong end. It is useless to try to relate

8 Ibid., p. 87.

arithmetic to savings and thrift, to interest and investment, if one does not consider life worth living to begin with, if the values of economy and investment have no significance. As a result, progressive education has tended to further a retreat into an anarchistic personalism in which the lonely ego seeks defenses against a vast impersonalism. To emphasize the meaninglessness of the whole, by explication or implication, is to force either total pessimism or unwarranted egocentricity on the lonely particular, man. He becomes, in modern terminology, consumption centered —no longer creative and productive, but concerned essentially with getting his share out of the whole meaningless mess.

In terms of such an outlook, algebra, science, history, and English are singularly irrelevant matters. Depending on one's personal inclinations, an interest can be cultivated in certain subjects but it is a purely subjective reaction. There is no sense of cultural necessity, no feeling that these skills constitute initiation into the life and culture of modern man and are hence indispensable. The sense of urgency in learning which the tribesman gives his son is lacking in our culture. We have created an imposing structure and declared its foundations to be irrelevant!

Here, the consistently Christian educator who has an epistemological self-consciousness is in a radically different position. He can teach in the confidence that there is a unity of learning in his school in that the ontological trinity is the presupposition of all factuality, and that all facts are created facts and hence God-given and consistent facts. He can avoid thereby the intellectual schizophrenia of our age, for himself and his students. However, if an ostensibly Christian teacher attempts to function on the alien presuppositions of ultimate impersonalism, then his tension and self-contradiction is the most radical of any. To "add" Christianity to an essentially alien curriculum, while more "respectable," is ultimately as phrenetic a step as the affirmation of a personalist faith in jazz. It is self-destructive and schizophrenic. A faith in a personal God cannot survive against the background of a world of impersonalism as portrayed in the average curriculum.

Parochial authority often maintains the Christian conformity of such schools, but they are none the less instruments of secularization, instruments in the furtherance of a world-view of ultimate pessimism and impersonalism. The coercive conformity of the parochial school masks the radical inner disunity, so that while it may at times offer better discipline, and more classical concepts of educational requirements, it nonetheless fails to give an *inner* unity to learning. And it is the *inner* unity of learning rather than an *outward* conformity to a common authority or standard which is our concern. This is not to disparage the value of true conformity, of course.

One of the most dangerous tendencies today, in any consideration of education, is to be seduced by the heady wine of nostalgia. Even as too much extraneous training is asked of the schools today, too much is ascribed to the schools of yesterday. Consider, for example, Clifton Fadiman's excellent and pointed account of his own high school education between 1916-1920. He attended an average school, with students all of whom would now be called "underprivileged," was taught a standard course which included four years of English, with rigorous drill in composition, grammar, and public speaking; four years of German; three years of French; three or four years of classical, European and American history, plus a course in civics, one year of physics; one year of biology; three years of mathematics, through trigonometry. All of this gave Fadiman a capacity for self-education. It also guaranteed that he would never be a member of a "lost" generation.[9] But why stop with Fadiman's day? Why not look back to Franklin, Massachussetts, more than a century earlier? Horace Mann, who despised the training he received, was in six months prepared for college by Samuel Barrett, genius and alcoholic, whom the tough Calvinists felt to be still a valid teacher, who gave more English grammar, Latin and Greek in his course than

[9] Clifton Fadiman, "Today's Lost Generation," pp. 13-15, 55 f., *Saturday Review,* Sept. 12, 1959, XLII, 37. This is adapted from Fadiman's introduction to James D. Koerner *The Case for Basic Education,* Boston, Atlantic Monthly Press, 1959.

collegians receive today. Mann mastered Latin grammar and read Corderius, Aesop's Fables; the Aeneid with parts of the Georgics and Bucolics; Cicero's Select Orations; the gospels and part of the epistles in Greek, and part of the Graeca Majora and Minora. What made Fadiman's education possible, and what made Mann's? Fadiman gives us an interesting insight into his schooling when he comments that, though underprivileged, his fellow students, coming from classes now producing "the largest quota of juvenile delinquents," were still so well behaved that the "one scandalous case" during his four years in high school involved the theft by a student of a pair of rubbers! Today, the most privileged public high school might be pleased to report no greater a student offense! And, with such a disciplined student body, who would not fail to teach more effectively? The child of Mann's day was definitely full of deviltry, often of a rougher sort, but he had a quick response to authority and recognized a responsibility to learn. This, in lesser form, existed in Fadiman's high school. The intense sense of responsibility of New England Calvinism is absent in modern youth. Granted the desirability of basic education, but will a change of curriculum alter the educational scene? After all, some of the teachers who today most conscientiously adhere to basic education often have, except with a few students, the most trying time. And, granted that some students have marked aptitudes, and take to solid study, how much substance is there to an education that rests on *aptitude* rather than exists as a *means to and necessity of life?* This approach of aptitude is an emphasis on permissiveness which is ultimately self-destructive. To be specific, here is the case of a young scientific technician, still in his middle twenties, already active in a highly promising career in advanced electronics, having had subsidized training and a guaranteed future. On the basis of aptitude, all this has been highly congenial. However, he has now discovered another aptitude which delights him even more, and being a member of an unrestricted and permissive generation, he boasts of it naively and with vicious pride. He is a successful male prostitute for women. Aptitude, certainly, is important, but, as an anarchistic principle, it is destructive and dangerous. Aptitude in itself conveys no standard, no law, no true framework of reference. The fallacy of nostalgia is that it tries to read into yesterday's education the latter-day effects and residue of American Puritanism, the ambitious self-discipline and imitative zeal of immigrant families, the now dead respect for "higher things" once common in a measure to all groups, the now decaying authority of the home, church, school, and society (as against the state), and so on. The courses Fadiman studied can be restored to the public high school, but the same students, with that same world behind them, can never be recalled. And, valuable as Fadiman's high school was to him, he is more definitely a product of that broader schooling.

What then is the answer? Are we to neglect matters of curriculum? Certainly not, but we must see them in their proper place and perspective. And, important as a catholic training in basic educational requirements may be, it is of far more importance to hold to a concept of the unity of learning. And it is the privilege of the consistent Christian that he can approach education without nostalgia, being committed, not to a point in the past, but to the development of Christian epistemological self-consciousness in the present and future. Churches indeed tend to look to an ideal past in terms of privilege, power, opportunity and success, but such nostalgia is a luxury which only the dying can afford. Let the dead therefore bury the dead; the living have work to do.

The Christian's concern is epistemological self-consciousness.[10] It is to declare that no fact is a fact apart from the ontological trinity, that all facts are personal facts precisely because they have been created by a personal God who alone is the true source of their interpretation, and that, because the whole created universe came into being by the act of that one God, whose eternal decree undergirds all reality, learning is not illusory and all learning has a fundamental unity.

[10] The implications of this will be developed subsequently.

4

The Kingdom of God and the School

The definitions of the home and the school are relatively simple matters. A very real problem, however, confronts us in the definition of the "church," a concept which must be understood if education is to be free. Here we find an area of considerable confusion, and some thinkers ready to assert conclusions unaware of their far-reaching implications. Again, Reformed thinkers have not always themselves been consistent to their insight here. The question is this: is the institutional church to be identified with the visible church? The Roman Catholic Church holds that the visible and invisible church are very closely linked and that the visible church is the institutional church. In other words, the Roman Catholic Church is the Kingdom of God on earth. The immediate implications of this for every-day life are far-reaching. The world is divided into two realms, first, the realm of grace, which is the Kingdom of God or the church, and, second, the realm of nature, which is the rest of the world. As a consequence, the only way in which the home, the school, and the government can be linked with God is through the institutional church, in that they possess no direct relationship with Christ and hence no direct relationship with God. Their relationship being mediated and subordinate to the institutional church, it becomes necessary for the state, school and home to be under the authority of the church in every avenue of life, and, as members of an inferior realm, the realm of nature, to be under constant suspicion and guard. The realm of nature is seen as in constant tension with the realm of grace and only able to serve God as it is dominated by the authority of grace, the church. Now as Dooyeweerd, Spier, Van Til, Vollenhoven and others have pointed out, this fundamental dichotomy between grace and nature is altogether unbiblical and wrong. The dichotomy is not between grace and nature but between grace and sin, so that when any realm of nature enters into the state of grace, it becomes part thereby of the visible church. To define the kingdom of God or the visible church in terms of the institutional church is to take the road to Rome, to drift toward the subordination of every avenue of life to the church. Many Protestants indeed share in this position and view every avenue of life with suspicion apart from ecclesiastical domination. But for us the biblical church, the kingdom of God on earth, is to be identified with the reign of God in the hearts of men wherever they are. Consequently, we must hold that the Christian home is a part of the visible church, as is the Christian school, the Christian state, and the Christian man in his calling, godly men everywhere in their calling serving as priests of the Kingdom of God on earth. The Christian as scientist manifests the activity of the visible church, of the Kingdom of God on earth, in his particular sphere of activity. The Christian farmer, as he subdues the earth and exercises dominion in the name of God is thereby manifesting the activity of the visible church in his particular sphere. Consequently, the *institutional* church is definitely not one area above all the other areas of life, but is one aspect of the Kingdom of God on earth among many others. For us, therefore, the *institutional* church together with and not above the school, the home, the Christian man in whatever calling or sphere of activity is his, equally represents the *visible* church, the Kingdom of God. The Christian school is a part of the visible church, and every school has a responsibility, if it be true to its function, to become a manifestation of the Kingdom. This entire concept has been well summarized by Spier, in his study of Dooyeweerd:

> If the visible church is equated with the church as an institution then the Roman Catholic dualism between "nature" and "grace" cannot be avoided. According to it, temporal life belongs to the sphere of nature. Christ is not the direct King of secular life. The sphere of faith is separate; it is a sphere of grace. Society is not a part of the body of Christ, but in its inner structure society is worldly and devoid of grace. It has its origin and end in temporal existence and, as such, does not lead to eternal life. The only tie that the sphere of nature can have with the sphere of Grace is indirect. Society can be bound only to Christ by grace. It can only approach God through the institution of the church. The latter alone can afford a haven for the sphere of nature. "Nature" is not "idle in the Lord," insofar as it is connected with the church. The latter cannot rest until it dominates human life in its entirety. If the consequences of the dualism between nature and grace are to be avoided, we must unequivocally maintain that the invisible church includes more than the institutional life of the church. The "visible" church is all of temporal society, insofar as it derives its life from Jesus Christ and employs its energy to advance His Kingdom. A Christian marriage, a Christian family, state, school, or any other Christian relationship which acknowledges Christ as the King of heaven and of earth, belongs to the visible church. Thus, the church as an institution, as a household of faith, is on the same level with all other relationships. The visible church, or the Kingdom of God, manifests itself in a multiplicity of forms, forms in which the Body of Christ is revealed. The church as an institution is not the revelation of the Body of Christ, but it is one revelation of it. The Body of Christ is revealed in other forms, (Compare Ephesians 5:23).[1]

[1] J. M. Spier: *An Introduction to Christian Philosophy*, p. 223. Philadelphia: Presbyterian and Reformed Publ. Co., 1954.

This point cannot be emphasized too strongly. The integrity of life depends upon it. In view of the confusion of many churches at this point, and their malpractice, the suspicion of many people with regard to the church is clearly justified.

In this view, the institutional church is limited to her task of proclaiming the Word of God to every creature, administering the sacraments to believers and their children, and governing herself in terms of the Word. The church to be a church must be a true church, a revelation of the Body of Christ.

The family is, sociologically and religiously, the basic institution, man's first and truest government, school, state, and church. Man's basic emotional and psychic needs are met in terms of the family. Man, the image of God, here exercises dominion as a priest in Christ, his wife a help-meet that he might fulfil his image mandate. The fifth commandment, calling for honor of parents, is properly in the first table of the law, being associated with Godward duties and the love of God. This direct association of honoring parents with obedience to God is apparent in the following laws:

Leviticus 19:3 "Ye shall fear every man his mother, and his father, and keep my sabbaths; I am the LORD, your God."

Exodus 21:15,17 called for death for smiting father, and for cursing father or mother. Cf. Leviticus 20:9.

Deuteronomy 21:18-21 called for the death penalty for incorrigible delinquents on complaint of the parents and confirmation by the local council.

Deuteronomy 22:20-25, Leviticus 20:10 The death penalty for adultery witnessed to the centrality of any offense against the home.

To disobey any true authority is to disobey God, but especially so with parents. Contempt of the home is a contempt of God, and rebellion against parents is associated with rebellion against God. Psychologically the two are linked. The typology of the home, its relationship typically to the fatherhood of God and to the headship of Christ over his church is deeply written in the constitution of man. Inevitably, rebellion against one is rebellion against the other. Thus the authority of the home is of tremendous significance.

In terms of all this, the significance of the Christian school begins to come into focus. The Christian school is a manifestation of the visible church, and at the same time, an extension of the home. It has therefore a relationship to God and to the visible church that makes it an intensely important and a central part of the church. The authority of the home, with its tremendous psychological relationship of the authority of the father to God, rebellion against the home equated with sabbath breaking and rebellion against God, carries over to the school. The school wields a power in the life of the child which it dare not use casually. For the child, the school is his world in a tremendous sense, and, if the school is not prepared to meet that heavy responsibility, it can do harm to the true church. To illustrate this, the child who begins school is convinced immediately that the teacher knows everything, often expressing surprise that the parents know as much as the teacher. The school thus is in a position to undermine other cultural agencies. The school is a world of authority and influence, in a very real sense representing the authority of God as a part of the visible church, and, again, the authority of the father, delegated. For a school to abuse its authority is to uproot a child in his religious and familist relationships and to produce a rootlessness of mind and personality devastating to both the person and his society. Unhappily, in too much of secular education this rootlessness is the hallmark of the successful student, and the more advanced the training the more radical the homelessness it produces. Education in this sense is anti-human and schizophrenic.

A particularly brilliant scholar, Dr. Eugen Rosenstock-Huessy, has spoken of the radical polytheism of modern life. Whereas a girl's faith was once monotheistic in that she shared the faith and was brought up under the authority of her father, having no other doctrines or values than his, now she is exposed in school and college to a variety of antagonistic creeds and doctrines. "A modern girl's education is polytheistic." Thus a man marries, not "one man's daughter, but many men's pupil," the product of "an unknown number of gods, deities, ideals, demons, powers." "Girls are exposed to a destruction of their sound instinct by all the false prophets of a golden-calf society."[2] We do live in an unquestionably polytheistic world, and, at every turn, art, education, press, television, movies, and state, press forward the claims of alien gods. At every corner we are face to face with a Baal demanding compliance or worship and the very complexity of modern life tempts many to concede to a polytheistic world.

This polytheism must be met. It cannot be met by retreat into a hopeless isolationism and retreat from the world. Neither can it be met by making common cause with polytheism, or by a surrender of any aspect of the Kingdom in the name of strategy. It can be met educationally, if the Christian school recognize the dimensions of the task and address itself to the problem. It cannot be an agency of withdrawal, nor of insulation, but rather of preparation in the recognition that the battle must be joined, that no person's life can escape the tensions of a polytheistic world, and that the answer is not in isolation but in conquest.

The Christian School, in dealing with the problem of polytheistic and rootless man, must deal with man in terms of the *heart* to avoid the contemporary atomization of man. While a particular subject may be strictly intellectual in its scope, the whole child is present in the school, and the assimilation of learning is in terms of the context of the whole.

The heart in romantic thought is equated with the emotions of man; romanticism has so thoroughly infiltrated modern thinking that this connotation has become almost inevitable for man today. An examination of the biblical concept of the heart gives us a radically different picture. Physiologically, the heart is the center of the body and the springs or issues of life physiologically

[2] Eugen Rosenstock-Huessy: *The Multiformity of Man*, pp. 58-60. Norwich, Vt., Beach head, 1949.

are out of the heart; it feeds, it nourishes, it keeps alive the whole body. It is spoken of in Scripture as the soul of the flesh: Lev. 17:11, "the soul of the flesh is in the blood." Again, in Gen. 9:4, Lev. 17:14, Deut. 12:23, we find the expression, "the blood is the soul." Thus, the blood is the soul of the flesh, and the heart is the physiological center of the blood, appropriating, assimilating, apportioning all things to the body. The spiritual heart of which Scripture speaks is analogous. The physical and the spiritual are closely linked and the center of the psychic soul, as differentiated from the soul of the flesh, is the heart. All spiritual life comes from this heart; it is the center of all willing and knowing. We are told of its diverse aspects and functions, to cite but a few instances:

1. Job 27:6, the source of conscience
2. Prov. 17:16, the source of intellect, knowing, moral discernment
3. I Kings 5:12, Prov. 10:8, wise heart
4. Psalm 51:12, pure heart
5. Genesis 20:5 f., honest and righteous heart
6. Psalm 10:4, perverse heart
7. Jeremiah 3:17, wicked and perverse heart
8. Ezekiel 38:2, haughty heart
9. Genesis 8:21, the source of evil
10. Jeremiah 17:9, desperately wicked
11. Deuteronomy 6:6, revelation is addressed to the heart
12. Lev. 26:41, Deut. 10:16, Ex. 4:21, wicked and uncircumcised heart
13. Deuteronomy 30:6, circumcise the heart
14. Psalms 33:11, 104:15, Gen. 8:21, Ex. 14:5, I Kings 8:33, Isa. 30:26, 66:14, Deut. 29:4, 4:9, source of intellectual and emotional life, of thought, memory, perception, will, imagination, joy, sorrow, anger, etc.
15. II Chron. 17:6, Ps. 37:1, Jer. 24:7, Deut. 11:13, I Kings 8:61, Jer. 32:40, the seat of religious feeling
16. Deut. 7:17, 8:17, 9:4, Isa. 14:13, the man himself, as against false fronts

17. I Peter 3:4, the heart is the hidden man, the real man
18. Ezekiel 36:26, "A new heart will I give you."

From these verses, it is apparent that regeneration does not mean that man is changed as far as his aptitudes are concerned; he remains the same man but with a new heart. Again, the inter-action and parallelism between body and spirit, or, more prop-erly, the fundamental unity between body and spirit is asserted, not merely a psychosomatic one but the reverse as well, so that the body can affect the heart and the heart the body. This is seen, for example in I Sam. 25:36,37, "Nabal's heart was very merry within him, for he was very drunken." Then again, "His heart died within him, and he became as stone." The body and the spirit being a unity share in their responses. Central to all this is the heart, out of which flow the springs of life (Prov. 4:23-27). In desert countries, the pollution of springs is a fearful crime, destroying life. The pollution of the springs of our life is held to be comparable, and is a spiritual and physical suicide in that the whole man is affected. Revelation speaks to the heart, and the true church or Kingdom in every realm rests on the foundation of a regenerated heart.

For secular education, the biblical concept of the heart is mythological, and much of secular education concerns itself ac-cordingly with the mind. This is particularly true of "basic edu-cation," which addresses itself to the mind of the child. Such education, as it has prevailed in much of the past history of edu-cation in the United States, has presupposed a predominantly rural country with no more radical divisions in the community than between Baptist and Presbyterian. The curriculum showed the impact of Christian concepts, and the Bible, read each day, was also the basic presupposition of all present. Such a back-ground for basic education no longer exists. It functions in iso-lation, in terms of the training and development of the mind of the child, and with the presupposition that the liberation of man is basically an intellectual affair, and that, socially, knowledge is power. This is an essentially religious position, and its consequences are a hastening of atomization and rootlessness. It is productive of an unhappy schizophrenia. A psychiatrist pinpointed this fact recently in calling attention to a representative case: a young woman who had been jilted just prior to her wedding had gradually developed serious personality disorders as a consequence. Her failure to cope with her problem was due directly to an intellectual fallacy. She had concluded that there was one mature, intellectual response only possible to her, in terms of an intellectual concept of the mature mind, and had accordingly denied herself the emotional response of indignation and anger. The consequence of that denial was the break-down of the whole person. The intellectual fallacy is a reduction of man to mind and the insistence that, not the heart, with its concept of wholeness, but the mind must be the man. As a result, there is the characteristic ambivalence of modern man between a sterile intellectualism and a phrenetic emotionalism. There is the intellectual denial of prejudices together with the intensified but suppressed emotional intensity of them. To return to the older form of basic education requires a cultural background which made possible the assumption of vast segments of learning and provided a common faith. Without that, basic education, while often ministering ably to the intellectual needs of the child in terms of subject knowledge, carries with it presuppositions of a dangerous sort. It is significant that basic education succeeds best where a stable background exists, or in Christian schools, where a basic faith gives wholeness in some measure.

On the other hand, progressive education, with its emphasis on educating the whole child, becomes immediately and inevitably a religious doctrine and a salvationist program. Its concern is inevitably soteric, involving a salvation and savior directly in contradiction to Christian faith. The plan of salvation is adjustment, the re-arrangement of the elements of society or of personality, but not a changed heart. It is a concept of social salvation, and no better description of it exists than *The Lonely Crowd*. The group, society, becomes the god, and morals become mores. The result is a radical alienation of the individual from himself.

The consequences of all this were apparent in Korean brain-washing. By separating man from himself and identifying him, not in terms of God but the group, by divorcing mind and emotions, and by denying the reality of the heart, man is unable to be himself and to retain his integrity as a man. To understand this, let us suppose ourselves a prisoner, being subjected to brain-washing. We are asked to write our autobiography and to include therein our attitude in 1939 to 1941 to the European War.[3] Let us assume that we were isolationists and so stated it. The immediate implication we would be confronted with would be the charge of pro-Hitlerism. It would be futile to defend ourselves, stating our anti-Hitler feelings, our anti-interventionism, or to assert the integrity of our heart. Our heart is a non-existent thing. Our moral principles are irrelevant. Activity alone matters, and in terms of this, we were in the wrong group and stand self-condemned. Christians alone were equipped to withstand consistently the implications of brainwashing. For them, the person was not an eroded concept, nor the intellectual fallacy a compelling one. Knowing that out of the heart are the issues of life, the Christian could face the social and intellectual fallacies with the confidence of his integrity before God.

The Christian school, because it does not work in a vacuum, is not under obligation to assume a total responsibility for the child. Because it is aware of the nature of the child, it can still work within its area with the total perspective in mind. This, of course, is true only if the school be theologically and philosophically aware of its true biblical presuppositions. Unhappily, this is too infrequently true even of theological seminaries. One

[3] This same method as applied in Soviet prisons, is described thus: "This process takes the form of an autobiography, written by the unbeliever (i.e., the non-conforming Marxist or anti-Marxist) in terms of the categories and the vocabulary of the believer (since the doctrine denies the existence of the spiritual life, the confession is exclusively concerned with actual conduct)." Raymond Aron: *The Opium of the Intellectuals*, p. 126. Garden City, N.Y. Doubleday, 1957.

of the amusing yet wretched facts about theological schools is their proneness to the intellectual or rational fallacy in the assumption that the logical sequence is the human sequence. Having been taught proper procedure in matters of administration or discipline, the young minister assumes that this is the true human procedure, with unhappy consequences! To equate man with his mind and to expect rational responses and results is no small fallacy, and yet it underlies too much thinking and acting today.

Inevitably, every educator today recognizes the religious implications of education and is drawn to the question of values, whether they be progressive or basic in their approach. Their dilemma is a real one. If a value be seen as objective, eternal and binding on all men, it leads ultimately to a limitation on man and an assertion of the eternal decree. If values are not objectively valid they are in essence only mores, the standards of the pack, and nothing more. And all education is in terms of a fundamental concept or faith which is in essence religious. The religious question has indeed been raised by the churches, and the public schools subjected to some challenge and pressure on that score. But it should be noted that, independent of all such activity, the schools themselves have insistently raised the religious issue, sometimes failing to identify it as such but nonetheless raising it. Again, various public groups have been insistent in raising the question.

The American Council on Education has urged a study of the question of religion in public education on the basis of the cultural crisis. "Religion is either central in human life or it is inconsequential."[4] "The spiritual replenishment of modern culture" requires capitalization of religious forces, and an attempt to meet the present crisis apart from such a measure is "sheer cultural madness."[5] The teaching of religion is thus a necessity. Our cul-

[4] The Committee on Religion and Education, American Council on Education: *The Relation of Religion to Public Education*, p. 53 Series I—Reports of Committees and conferences—No. 26. Washington, D.C. Vol. II, April, 1947.
[5] *Ibid.*, p. 46 f.

ture having a "Judeo-Christian" foundation, its continued existence requires revitalization in terms of those basic beliefs which
nurture its life. But how is religion to be taught? The "common
core of religious belief" concept is clearly rejected as fallacious.
Such an attempt would lead only to the creation of a new religion, "a public school sect—which would take its place along-
side the existing faiths and compete with them."[6] That religion
in the schools would offend some is recognized. On the other
hand, what concept will not? Equality is taught in schools with
fewer believers than Christianity but taught because the nation
feels committed to it as part of the "democratic ideal." The absolute separation of church and state is an impossibility, and the
Constitution separates the *institution* rather than the *faith*. Again,
religion is taught, albeit anti-Christian religion, under other
names. "To call supernaturalism a religion and naturalism a philosophy and on that basis to exclude the one and embrace the
other is, we think, a form of self-deception."[7] The basic responsibility of the public schools is that they have an obligation to give
the young an understanding of the mainspring of our culture and
its standards. But it cannot be a merely objective study. To approach the subject of religion as though it were a matter of
neutrality or indifference "is to be unneutral—to weight the
scales against any concern with religion."[8] Without being committed to a sectarian position, the public school must give importance to the reality of specific commitment and give pupils
opportunity for independent study. The problem is a difficult
one, requiring trained teachers and the cooperation of the
churches with the program, but, religion being inseparably bound
up with the culture as a whole, the problem must be met.

This is an important and sensitive study of the question and
yet, like others, has not been fruitful. The one answer not faced
is the abolition of the public school system. There is an implicit

[6] *Ibid.*, p. 15.
[7] *Ibid.*, p. 20.
[8] *Ibid.*, p. 29.

medievalism here that needs attention. The Christian is constantly told that he must face up to the fact of a pluralistic world, and rightly so. Theologically, it is erroneous to expect a common cultural picture, and any theology operating on that basis needs to be suspect. The progression of time and the epistemological development of history require a growing self-consciousness which will emphasize pluralism. There are churches, and liberal Protestantism with its social gospel ideas of the Kingdom of God and church union is prominent among them, which work for a new medievalism, a monolithic culture with an organized culture. But, more than ever before, our world cannot trust such a monolithic power of control to anyone, nor aspire to such an enforced concept of culture. Pluralism must be accepted, and the best hope of man in true culture seen in free and pluralistic terms. *The public school is a substitute institution for the Holy Roman Empire and the Roman Catholic Church of the middle ages and is a thoroughly medieval concept. A single culture is demanded, and the public school must create it. Hence, every group believing in and seeking to control that new leviathan and grand monolith seeks control of the public school.* But a free and pluralistic society requires the abolition of the public school and the tax support of the school in favor of a pluralistic education. The competitive aspect will ensure the quality of education, and the cultural implications of various faiths, philosophies and opinions can be given freedom to develop and make their contribution. Our society today, despite its pretensions, is not pluralistic except with regard to religion, which it considers a matter of indifference. In all else, it is monolithic. The orthodox Christian can face a pluralistic society in the confidence that his faith can, given such freedom, establish its power and superiority culturally and religiously. He must realize that today agnosticism has secured the status of an established church by means of the institution of the public school, and this new religion must be disestablished.

Another consideration of the problem of religion and education comes from the "Rockefeller Report" on Education whose primary concern was with education and the individual. According to the report the ultimate source of greatness in a nation is the greatness of its individuals. Only a free society can give the individual the opportunity to develop his potentialities. The central value is the "overriding importance of human dignity. It is not a means but an end. It expresses our notion of what constitutes a good life and our ultimate values."[9] The report is aware of the conflict between equality and excellence and resolves it in terms of the limitation of equality to mean equal opportunity and equal status before the law. To insist on a radical concept of equality is to force even more serious inequalities on society. A recognition of basic values is imperative in education; science, for example, needs integrity if society is to have integrity. Federal aid to education is assumed irreversible. Finally, the question of values is faced, and it is recognized as essential to the future of our culture. Every value today is subject to danger and survival requires that values be fought for. But what are they? The answer is a remarkable one:

> We would not wish to impose upon students a rigidly defined set of values. Each student is free to vary the nature of his commitment. But this freedom must be understood in its true light. We believe that the individual should be free and morally responsible: the two are inseparable. The fact that we tolerate differing values must not be confused with moral neutrality. Such tolerance must be built upon a base of moral commitment; otherwise it degenerates into a flaccid indifference, purged of all belief and devotion.
>
> In short, we will wish to allow wide latitude in the choice of values, but we must assume that education is a process that should be infused with meaning and purpose; that everyone will have deeply held beliefs; that every young American will wish

[9] Special Studies Project Report V. Rockefeller Brothers Fund: *The Pursuit of Excellence, Education and the Future of America*, p. 3. Garden City, N.Y. Doubleday, 1958.

to serve the values which have nurtured him and made possible his education and his freedom as an individual.[10]

A clearer demonstration that intelligence is not necessarily productive of sense could hardly be desired! The only thing such an education can teach is the total social irrelevance of all values. In such a concept, what is the individual "morally responsible" to? Since the ultimate goal and the "end" is the "overriding importance of human dignity," what other value can exist, or compare with it? Is not this rather education into undiluted egoism? And is it not precisely the moral neutrality they wish to avoid? Every man is his own god and the ultimate arbiter of value. Let neither law nor education dare to interfere with this "overriding importance" and sanctity of man.

Lacking the transcendental standard which Scripture provides, other systems inevitably turn to an immanent one and absolutize the state, the individual, or some other aspect of life. Russell Kirk has raised the pertinent question: "Can there be an end or aim to anything without a religious interpretation of life?"[11] For many today who claim to be irreligious, their god is, as Kirk states, Demos. These immanent gods of the modern world create an absolute authority on the human level, which, in the name of those gods, whether communism, democracy, liberty or equality, manifests a demand for totalitarian obedience. The university, as Kirk demonstrates, seeks the same kind of obedience in its realm to its own particular immanent gods.

The only safeguard against all this is a consistent, biblical faith. This means that the institutional church cannot be identified with the totality of the church or the Kingdom of God and thereby made that order incarnated or manifested in history. Moreover, the authority of the church must be biblical, strictly *ministerial*, and never *legislative*, in terms of the will and purpose of God as manifested in Scripture. The authority of the church

[10] *Ibid.*, p. 49.
[11] Russell Kirk: *Academic Freedom, An Essay in Definition*, p. 49. Chicago: Regnery, 1955.

is in the area of the proclamation of the word of God, the administration of the sacraments, and the government of its own inner life as an institution. Christianity destroys itself if it absolutizes an immanent authority.

There has been another attempt to solve the contemporary dilemma that needs mention. The "beatnik" interest in Zen Buddhism is a manifestation of it. It is an attempt to find a new source of meaning for life and society by evading the whole issue of religion, of meaning, in favor of aesthetics. Oriental culture some centuries ago lost all faith in the concept of truth, found relativism to be a deadly doctrine in its naked form, and took refuge in aestheticism, in beauty as a substitute for truth. The result was a long eclipse and stagnation now rapidly being set aside for Western absolutist concepts, usually Marxism, sometimes Christianity, often other philosophical alternatives. The idea has not been without its appeal to Western man and has appeared in partial form in pragmatism, so that Eugen Rosenstock-Huessy, in his perceptive study of *The Christian Future*, speaks of it as "our invasion by China." But pragmatism has been inevitably religious and has merely substituted new absolutes for older ones. The process of withdrawal from the concept of truth described by George Sansom in *A History of Japan to 1334* requires an aristocratic luxury and isolation which, while some writers have sought, modern life does not permit. The beatnik, the "happy" and "blessed" man by his own definition, seeks to find this life of beatitude in an isolation of self from all responsibility, value, meaning, and truth, only to find himself in isolation from life and in effect a lover of death. As the world grows more complex, the demands of life become more implacable even as its promises abound. In the face of all this, our confidence is that the God who created it, and ordained that we should be kings over creation, will guide, sustain, and prosper us as we work in conformity to His mandate and in terms of His Word.

5

The State and Education

Some years ago Lowie described the education of "primitive" peoples as utilizing, among other things, social pressure, ridicule, group example, and social expectation.[1] This is effective in tribal culture, where one unchallenged way of life exists. There are many, however, who feel that modern man has much to learn from "primitives," and some of the most absurd of studies have been undertaken in this spirit. This imitative concern is hardly necessary, however, in that the modern concern with *the group* and with *mankind as a whole* has been productive of a new tribalism in modern man. Whether the tribe includes all of mankind, our state, or is a nomadic band of fifty persons, it remains a tribe in this restrictive sense, if the individual members refuse a personal sense of responsibility, supplant objective and eternal law with tribal law (as the Supreme Court has done), and find nothing more distasteful than being a man. All reality and power is given to the pack and self-consciousness apart from the pack

[1] Robert H. Lowie, *Are We Civilized?* pp. 167-178, New York, Harcourt, Brace, 1929.

54

seen as a sickly phenomenon. The pack is a "lonely crowd" and all its integration an exercise in futility, in that manhood remains an inescapable reminder and reality. One of the early prophets of the modern mood asserted,

> I think I could turn and live with animals, they are so placid and
>   self-contain'd;
> I stand and look at them long and long.
> They do not sweat and whine about their condition;
> They do not lie awake in the dark and weep for their sins;
> They do not make me sick discussing their duty to God;
> Not one is dissatisfied—not one is demented with the mania of
>   owning things;
> Not one kneels to another, nor to his kind that lived thousands
>   of years ago;
> Not one is respectable or industrious over the whole earth.[2]

Notice that this catalogue of sins actually amounts to one sin, *manhood*. Discontent with one's condition alone brings material progress; discontent with one's spiritual state alone brings repentance and new life. Duty to God is the privilege of humanity not a sickness. Private property ("owning things") is no "mania" but an essential part of the development of freedom and the personality of man. To worship is to know God, and oneself in relationship to Him. And to be "respectable or industrious" is hardly a sin in any society! But Whitman wrote of these things with real revulsion and found it better to be an animal than a man. His sentiments have been widely echoed. The essence of manhood is responsibility, and a rebellion against responsibility means a rebellion against the condition of being human. It is a desire to be as God and yet with no more responsibility for thought and action than a "placid" animal. The "lonely crowd" is sick of responsibility. Much of modern education encourages a socialization of standards, tastes, interests, and experiences. In all of this, is the public school the architect or the victim?

Before answering that question, let us examine what Van Til

[2] Walt Whitman's poem "Walt Whitman," 32, from *Leaves of Grass*.

has called "integration into the void."[3] Psychology began its recent history by rebelling against the domination of man by intellect and turned to irrationalism. A further step was child psychology, and the attempt to read the man in terms of the child. The adult was together with the child next read in terms of the unconscious. Further steps towards integration into the void were taken by studies in the psychology of "primitive" man and then of animals. That modern psychology is deeply imbued with the Romantic revolt against reason and is part of the same impulse is clearcut. But equally apparent is the fact that truth has given way to relativism, and the concept of man has been eroded into nothingness. Thus the integration into the void is part and parcel of the larger revolt against God. But the inevitable outcome is this: No God, no man.

Culturally, education has been an initiation into life and a declaration of the meaning and means of life, and the school has been one instrument in this task. But society can never give what it does not possess, and modern man possesses no image of man which gives function and structure to society. Moreover, education has passed into the hands of the state, a major step. Although, in the United States, this transfer of education to the state began early in the 1800's, in actuality it was not in full effect until after World War I. Prior to the early 1800's, schools had been operated by churches, local parents, or by the teachers. Higher education maintained its religious orientation much later. In 1860 all but 17 of the universities and colleges in the United States were under church control. Until modern means of communication revolutionized the nation, the public school, while actually a state school, was largely under local control and extensively given to religious influence. The pressure now is steadily towards the elimination of local control entirely, and the securing of federal aid to education to supplement state and county funds.

[3] For Van Til's account of this see *The Psychology of Religion*, or R. J. Rushdoony, in the "Psychology of Religion: Integration into the Void," pp. 65-80, in *By What Standard?*

The public school is now unmistakably a state school, and its concept of education is inevitably statist. This is apparent in various ways. First of all, education has ceased to be a responsibility of the home and has become a responsibility of the state. Even if the parents are better able to educate their children than the state, as in the William and Mary Turner case in California, the state still claims sole right to determine the nature, extent, and time of education. Thus, a basic family right has been destroyed and the state's control over the child asserted. Second, education is now coercive. Attendance is compulsory up to a certain age. The result is destructive of the educational process, in that the captive students slow down and wreck the educative methods. To cite a specific example, a junior high school boy attempted to knife a teacher but was not expelled, although this was one of a long series of violent acts. The child would have welcomed expulsion, so it was no punishment. The courts had too many more serious offenders in hand, and no room for more, and the police felt that the best place for such a boy was at home and in school. As a result, until he reaches 16, this boy will continue to make a havoc of his classes, and the teachers will be compelled to submit. Coercion has its place in society and is often a needed thing, but, in terms of education, it is destructive when the state uses coercion to compel attendance. Without coercion, the loss in numbers would be negligible but the educational gains incalculable. Third, by making the school dependent on government funds, taxes, instead of the people, the school is converted into another institution dedicated to self-advantage rather than to its function. The last forty years have seen far more advance in school facilities and funds than in successful education. The psychology of state schools is no different than that of state churches, a belief that they are the sole means of truth, a high insolence towards the critic, and a progressively fat inefficiency.

A statist school, moreover, has no concept of truth to offer. Some of the most appalling instances of this have come from prominent scholars genuinely concerned over the claimed superiority of Russian science. Their demands for better education are understandable, but their nakedly statist reasons are not. But, it can be objected, is not survival the issue? Is the issue survival, or is it truth? To survive, must we become socialist (as we are in rapid process becoming), and must we adopt statist concepts for life and education? Is education a function of statist man or of true and whole man? Education, if it becomes statist or parochial, then reflects the ends of an institution, although a redeeming factor with the church is that ideally and sometimes actually it points beyond itself to God. In either instance, however, education tends to become limited in scope, and in statist education especially limited to the narrow purposes of the state.

The question is often raised, can the "private" school survive? The more basic question needs to be raised: has the statist school any right to survive? Educators who advocate state schools do so in the name of the state and a common state culture; they may use less plain speech, but their meaning is the same. The irony here is that these same men, in arguing against the need for a common religious faith, insist on a pluralist society, but in dealing with education and the state, and a common culture, they are militantly anti-pluralist. The answer is, of course, that the area of pluralism is the area of peripheral values; in things essential, they are far more rigid than medieval man in their insistence on conformity to the new see of St. Peter, the state and its culture.

Statist education has, moreover, been singularly unable to give any true sense of direction or purpose, or a concept of growth. As Van Til has commented, "Education on Dewey's basis is merely animal growth."[4] Let us consider, for example, the attempt of the National Education Association to formulate a statement of purpose, direction, and growth in education. Written by Charles A. Beard, revised by the Educational Policies Commission, and published in 1937, we have here a considered

---

[4] C. Van Til: *The Dilemma of Education*, p. 13. Phila.: Presbyterian and Reformed, 1954.

statement of *The Unique Function of Education in American Democracy.* Its "five guiding principles" to which the educator "must . . . refer in discovering the task of education in American democracy" emphasize relativism. The school is linked with the state rather than an antiquarian interest in knowledge as such.

> Public education is anchored in the nature of civilization as unfolded. It is thus closely associated with the ideals, policies, and institutions of government and economy, as well as the arts and sciences. Although some forms of private education may be far removed from the hard world of practice, public education can maintain no such isolation. Many professional representatives, it is true, may properly concentrate on schoolroom procedure, methods, and testing, but the leaders who determine the content and objectives of instruction must work under the immediate impacts of society—its needs, drives, and demands.[5]

> So viewed, the association of educational history with the encompassing history of American civilization is not a form of antiquarianism and dust-sifting. On the contrary by this process alone does it seem possible to obtain sure guidance in the formulation of an educational policy corresponding to the realities of the living present, now rising out of the past.[6]

In one sense, this sounds both innocent and commendable, and really unnecessary to say. After all, education is a human activity and is inescapably relevant. And the school Clifton Fadiman attended had a definite relationship to life and society. What then is the drift of all this? "Antiquarianism and dust-sifting" in education is failure to attempt to remake man and his society.

In dealing with ethics, the Commission was all for guarding "those virtues of the race" common to "the humblest" such as "industry, patience, self-denial and consideration for others" (all of which sound a little uncommon), as well as "the imperial gifts of imagination, originality, and invention." Education is important because it "nourishes the underlying values upon which

[5] N.E.A., *The Unique Function of Education in American Democracy,* p. 66f. Washington: N.E.A., 1937.
[6] *Ibid.,* p. 69.

State and Society depend for their existence." The greatest obligation of education is "to truth in itself and for its own sake—obligations to seek it, defend it, and make humane use of it." What truth means, we are not told, or if truth is more than a relative concept; this latter seems to be inferred.[7] Later, however, ethics and truth seem to be equated with the important but not binding experiences of the past. Education "needs" ethics because it "embraces knowledge, training, and aspirations." "The primary business of education, in effecting the promises of American democracy, is to guard, cherish, advance, and make available in the life of coming generations the funded and growing wisdom, knowledge, and aspirations of the race."[8] Thus, the basic faith is in democracy, as the statement then repeatedly demonstrates, and there is no higher value. In terms of this, propaganda and education are defined. The Commission was aware that its definition of education made it appear to be no more than state propaganda. Here, democracy came to the rescue. There is a difference between influencing human behavior if it is done for that great Leviathan, Democracy, and between such activity on the part of a group. Thus propaganda "is an instrument of a faction or a party." Moreover, it is partial in its picture, not giving other positions a hearing, which, apparently, democratic education does.[9]

We are given more information by the N.E.A. on *The Purposes of Education in American Democracy*. Ethics is emphasized, but not in any traditional sense. It is essentially altruism in the sense of serving humanity. The best means of teaching is implicit in method; a school which is autocratic can bring "no lasting contribution to peace, reason, and order," nor can a school emphasizing competition, or personal advancement do its part in this cause. "Only from methods of instruction which not only teach but which actually *are* democracy and cooperation, will

[7] *Ibid.*, pp. 71-73.
[8] *Ibid.*, pp. 77-82.
[9] *Ibid.*, p. 99f.

the appeal to reason be heard and heeded."[10] The educational purposes are four-fold: the objectives of self-realization, human relationship, economic efficiency, and civic responsibility. In speaking of "character," it is said that "The educated person gives responsible direction to his own life."[11] But all people give "responsible direction" to their lives. The point is, responsible to what? The answer is definitely not God in any supernatural sense. Supernaturalism is a gross business which leads to persecution and the applause of "the most vicious depravity and the most selfish exploitation." After this astounding verdict on orthodox Christianity, we are further told, "Although such a philosophy may be satisfactory to its possessor, it is definitely unsatisfactory to others." And that, of course, is condemnation enough from this democratic perspective. True ethics is self-born and is congenial "to self-realization through democratic processes."[12] What follows then is a call for the re-ordering of all aspects of life and the world itself in terms of this democratic and levelling perspective.

With the details of these two statements, educators are no longer in agreement; with regard to their basic premises, there is no change. Education has no reference beyond democratic man, no concept of growth, truth, or meaning of any objective validity. The consequences of such a position are well described by Helmut Schoeck as the destruction of the desired individuality by the lust for equality.[13]

The state is an important institution, an indispensable and God-ordained institution, but it is not creative, nor is it productive. Only as the state is limited to its proper jurisdiction (and the same is true of the church), can society be free and productive. Art, science, church, school, family, business, agriculture, every-

[10] N.E.A. Educational Policies Commission, *The Purposes of Education in American Democracy* p. 31f., Washington, N.E.A., 1938.

[11] *Ibid.*, p. 50.

[12] *Ibid.*, pp. 68-71.

[13] Helmut Schoeck, "Individuality vs. Equality," pp. 103-124, in Felix Morley, ed., *Essays on Individuality.*

thing can then function freely in order that man might fulfil his calling under God. The state cannot give meaning or function; it must itself derive meaning and direction from a free society under God, one able to realize itself in terms of its image mandate. If the state assumes authority and jurisdiction in the various realms, it chokes off their true development, because the state can only give them subsidies, never meaning. Accordingly, the public school, in trying to assist the state and become a fellow-architect of the statist culture, has victimized itself. Like a variety of other recipients of subsidy, it fawns on the feeding hand, scarcely aware that it is being fattened for the state's own purposes. And now "private" schools, colleges and universities have found their way, through various grants, to the generous trough and are hungry for more, too often hungry, indeed, for everything except the radical independence of education from the state.

Dooyeweerd, in insisting on the vital relationship of family and school as against state and school, has observed that "the ancient and modern totalitarian ideas of State education of the children contradicts the divine world-order and are indeed inhuman and destructive to human society."[14]

A rise in the power of the state is the beginning of the breakdown of meaning and community and the social descent into hell. The biblical doctrine of hell is a necessary if much misunderstood concept. The final and eternal state of hell is not presented as a society, because society is an aspect of the internal relationship of the triune God and is therefore progressively impossible in isolation from God, an impossibility in hell. Hell is the totality of frustration and meaninglessness, and this is its torment and burning, its weeping, wailing and gnashing of teeth. It is without government or knowledge, because with total epistemological self-consciousness apart from God there is a total rejection of knowledge and meaning.

Hell today haunts the boundaries of modern life and appears even in its "good life," its play and love, with its mocking frus-

14 Herman Dooyeweerd, *A New Critique of Theoretical Thought,* III, p. 288.

tration and collapse of meaning. Hell awaits culture after culture, as, torn by its inner tensions and schizophrenia, it collapses into frustration and evasion. Man's culture apart from God is in continual crisis, and the promise is that, with the rising tensions, men's hearts shall indeed fail them for fear because of the meaninglessness of their efforts and the crises which shatter human endeavors (Luke 21:26). Because meaning cannot exist apart from God, education too is haunted by the same spectre of emptiness. All creation witnesses to the glory of God, and all creation and all factuality witnesses against the man and culture who flee from Him. According to Deborah, who wrote out of no easy circumstances, "the stars in their courses fought against Sisera" (Judges 5:20). Life is no different now, still a battle, but with this assurance always, that the very course of creation works to confirm and establish that man whose life is given to the glory of God and that pursuit of knowledge which is consistent with Him by whom all things are known.

Note 1 to Chapter 5

The Religion of the Public Schools

In 1951 the Educational Policies Commission of the N.E.A. issued its statement on *Moral and Spiritual Values in the Public Schools* (written by William G. Carr) with the expressed hope "that this report will encourage in homes, churches, and schools a nationwide renaissance of interest in education for moral and spiritual values" (vi). It declared, "By moral and spiritual values we mean those values which, when applied to human behavior, exalt and refine life and bring it into accord with the standards of conduct that are approved in our democratic culture" (p. 3). Thus the group is still the source of values. The voice of the people is fully the voice of God. Schools and teachers must serve the people; they cannot serve any supernatural God, and "They can have no part in securing acceptance of any one of the numerous systems of belief regarding a supernatural power and the relation of mankind thereto"; but we are told that very high spiritual and moral values are possible apart from supernaturalism and are taught by the public schools (p. 4). The public schools are not against religion. Rather, "The public schools of the United States, stand firmly for freedom of religious belief." A common education must be given based on a "respect" for all religious opinions. "Such an education must be derived, not from some synthetic patchwork of many religious views, but rather from the moral and spiritual values which are shared by the members of all religious faiths. Such education has profound religious significance" (p. 6). A more beggarly concept is hardly possible. Here is the old myth of the common core of religion at the heart of all religions. It is comparable to saying that we must hold to a respect for monarchy, fascism, naziism, communism, feudalism, republicanism and democracy and believe in the moral and spiritual values shared by all of them. It would be to affirm a belief in government as such as being moral, irrespective of its character. Religion as such can be true or false, good or bad, decadent or virile. *To affirm religion as such is to affirm the irrelevance of all moral and spiritual values,* and this is the true implication of this stand taken by the Educational Policies Commission.

This is clearly apparent in the developed concept of values. Values are not transcendent, least of all derived from God. Human personality is "the basic value," and the individual is capable of acquiring all needed values. "This doctrine sharply challenges every form of oppression" (p. 18 f.). Autonomous man needs no external forces to attain self-realization, a concept of values, or moral and spiritual competence.

In terms of this, the public school claims to teach religion and states that it needs partners. That it teaches religion, we must grant, but we must insist that this religion is anti-Christianity and that no concept of Christianity which tries to conform to the biblical standards can ever give approval to the religion of the public schools. What the public schools claim is a neutral concept of religion is indeed a concept of neutrality with regard to truth and cannot be allowed to go unchallenged by all who believe truth to be important.

A further comment on the values of democratic culture can be made. It is hostile to that which emphasizes the basically isolating inner issues and is a culturally limited experience, that is, beyond the appreciation of more than a segment of the population. Notice this comment in the 1938 document, *Purposes of Education in American Democracy:* "It is at least open to question whether there is anything intrinsically more dramatic and elevating in watching the struggle on a darkening stage between Macbeth and his conscience than in watching under a warm summer sun a good nine-inning pitching duel" (p. 65). In view of such standards, we have no cause for surprise at the results of education.

Note 2 to Chapter 5

The Presbyterian Church U.S.A. and the Public Schools

On May 20, 1957 the General Assembly of the Presbyterian Church in the United States of America (since become the United Presbyterian Church in the United States of America) received and adopted a statement entitled "The Presbyterian Church in the United States of America and the Public Schools."[1] This document in itself has no importance except as the self-conscious statement of "a main artery of Protestantism, concerning the nature and aims of public education among a few people." A main, if hardened, artery needs to be listened to!

The basic weakness of the statement is that it rests primarily, not on an articulate and consistent faith or philosophy, but on a fear of Roman Catholicism and its claims to tax funds for parochial schools. Had the report dealt squarely with this issue as such, it might have had more consistency.

[1] The report, also reprinted separately, appeared in the *Minutes of the General Assembly of the Presbyterian Church in the U.S.A.* Fifth Series—vol VI—1957, Parts I and II pp. 93-118.

The statement denies that the public schools are "godless," and yet strikes at "The Common Core or Residuum of Common Agreements" idea in the clearest passage in the entire report. The "common core" of religion idea, as it appears in public schools, is false in that "religious commitment arises in a specific and concrete religious community, highly articulate, and never abstracted into common elements." Thus, there can be no countenancing of "the teaching of devitalized 'common faith' as a proper substitute for highly specific religious belief (II, c, 2). But this dilemma is never resolved. The public schools, implicitly or explicitly, assert a system of values hostile to Christianity. How is the church to reconcile itself with this reality?

The apparent solution is in a Thomistic answer to the question of truth. Religious knowledge requires supernatural revelation and the Holy Spirit, whereas natural revelation can be validly seen by the light of reason. "The public school may well provide a context for growth in understanding which does no violence to the validity of revelation. Indeed, the public school can make valuable contributions to man's understanding of true revelation by increasing literacy and general comprehension of the nature of knowledge" (I, c, 2). Rome has nothing to fear from an artery which has so far altered its Reformed pulse as to carry a Thomistic nature. The statement insists on "the divine origin of all values" but not on the divine creation and interpretation of all factuality, a concept which would destroy its premise for public schools (II, c, 1).

The public school has, moreover, a central value all its own. It is democratic, and the child, no matter how valuable his "private" school training may be in other respects, must not be "isolated" from the "main stream" or encouraged in "cloistered living." There is some especial virtue in the togetherness of democratic public schools which 'private' Christian or parochial schools, no matter how representative their student bodies, are assumed to lack. Apparently it is participation in that sacred mystical body, the State. And apparently a common religious faith among the students is a handicap rather than an asset and strength.

Note 3 to Chapter 5

The State and Liberal Education

In a thoughtful and persuasive collection of essays, President Griswold of Yale states the case for liberal education, not as a universal prescription but as a necessary element in truly free education. As he points out, "liberal arts" properly means "the arts becoming to a free man." Liberal education is directly related to knowledge, freedom and civilization. "Not only does it concern itself more directly and vitally than any other type of education with the good life that is the end of all political society; it also shows a like concern for the means whereby that society is to be governed and the good life achieved."[1] The basis of all rule of law is in character and in morality.

> The moral, then, is plain. To do good we must first know good; to serve beauty we must first know beauty; to speak the truth we must first know the truth. We must know these things ourselves, be able to recognize them by ourselves, be able to describe, explain, and communicate them by ourselves, and wish to do so, when no one else is present to prompt us or bargain with us. Such knowledge is the purpose of liberal education. We must hold true to that purpose. No price, no mess of pottage, can equal its value to our country and ourselves, its citizens.[2]

The unhappy fact about this eloquent statement is that it concludes the book rather than opens up the problem. As a result, the issue posed here in never met.

A sadder fact confronts us as we examine Griswold's conception of the good life; it is "the end of all political society," a definition increasingly common in the last two centuries (as it

---

[1] A. Whitney Griswold: *Liberal Education and the Democratic Ideal and Other Essays,* p. vi. New Haven, Yale U. Press, 1959.
[2] *Ibid.,* p. 136.

was in areas of the ancient world, as witness the Greek states,)
but by no means the basic concept in Western culture. That a
free state is important in the good life is granted, but men have
known the good life without it. The basic definition of the good
life has been in terms of God and man's freedom under God, a
freedom from the burden of guilt and sin and the ability to fulfil
his image mandate as God's vicegerent. There was a time at
Yale when the good life would have been defined thus: "The
chief end of man is to glorify God and to enjoy Him forever."
Griswold is troubled by the growth of state power, but he has
no weapon against it, since for him the good life is defined in
terms of it. Moreover, he agrees with Jefferson in calling education "the most legitimate engine of government" and thereby
surrendering the independence of that area which is ostensibly
to undergird freedom. How much he concedes to the state appears in his essay on "The Limited Competence of the State."
The preservation of democracy he finds in the principle of the
"separation of powers." The checks and balances in the United
States have been endangered in recent years. But separation of
powers means also that the realm of the spirit was reserved to
the church, and the realm of mind to the school. This is the
"sacred maxim of free government," and, apparently, sacred to
nothing more. Griswold is too conscious of modern skepticism
to assert any God-given rights here, or 'natural' rights. The wisdom of the founding fathers so ordered it. He accepts it historically and values it personally. He establishes no principle whereby the integrity of any realm stands. And, since the good life
is in terms of the state, no area can ultimately withstand the
sovereign claims of the state, since it apparently exists by the
indulgence and grace of the state. Since the good life is political,
Griswold is ready to believe that "the voice of the people is the
voice of God."[3] But the state, unhappily is a Moses who can only
lead these chosen people into the wilderness, never out of it.

[3] *Ibid.,* p. 99.

6

The Concept of the Child

The child is not only a person but a concept, in that each culture has its own particular idea and expectation of a child. Thus the concept of the child in a culture motivated by ancestor worship is radically different from that of today. The child is born into a culture and is loved and honored as it meets the expectations of that culture.

What then is the modern cultural concept of the child? Dingwall has called attention to the emphasis in the United States on the "purity" and "innocence" of the child, and the prevalence of the idea of "the child as the hope of the future."[1] Dingwall is incorrect in regarding this as an exclusively American aberration, in that Great Britain is also given to such thinking. Hemming and Balls, in *The Child is Right,* can hold that "we adults hold in our hands the future happiness, character and achievement of our country . . . A child is not 'born in sin,' it is not 'full of the old Adam,' it is a bundle of living, willing, thinking, sensitive flesh, neutral as to good or evil . . . and it is utterly in the hands

[1] Eric John Dingwall: *The American Woman,* p. 123. New York: Signet Bks., 1958.

of grown ups."[2] The purity and innocence of the child is seen basically as a moral neutrality. The child is passive and to be shaped.

This runs directly counter to the older Protestant concept of the child as (1) a creature fearfully and wonderfully made in the image of God, and with awesome responsibilities, and yet (2) conceived in sin, that is, born with a predisposition to sin, in original sin, which radically tainted every aspect of his being. "In Adam's fall, we sinned all," New England school children were once taught. In this concept, in terms of this twofold aspect of the child, education involved two fundamental facts, first, education into the grave dignity and responsibilities of one created in God's image, and, second, discipline in the realization that this responsibility could not be met unless the old Adam was mortified. This attitude long colored education. It lingered long in the United States and elsewhere in curriculum content, in the moral emphasis in readers. Longfellow's "Psalm of Life" summed up this educational goal, prevalent and influential long after Protestant orthodoxy receded:

> Life is real! Life is earnest!
> And the grave is not its goal
>
> . . . .
>
> In the world's broad field of battle,
> In the bivouac of Life,
> Be not like dumb, driven cattle!
> Be a hero in the strife!
>
> . . . .
>
> Let us, then, be up and doing,
> With a heart for any fate;
> Still achieving, still pursuing,
> Learn to labor and to wait.

[2] From Hemming and Balls: *The Child is Right,* p. 3, cited in E. W. Crabb: *Train up a Child,* p. 63, London: Paternoster, 1954. The English Romantics exceeded American thinkers in their exaltation of the child. Somewhat later, we find Martin Farquhar Tupper, for example, stating, in his *Proverbial Philosophy,* "A Babe in a house is a well spring of pleasure, a messenger of peace and love: A resting place for innocence on earth; a link between angels and men; Yet is it a talent of trust, a loan to be rendered back with interest . . ." (1847).

Countless children memorized and recited these lines as a part of classwork and learned both to labor and to wait. But children brought up on a concept of life, not as battle but play, and with an emphasis on their needs, can neither labor nor yet wait.

For the emphasis now is on the *needs* of the child, not on the *demands and expectations* of the culture. Once the literature of youth abounded in an emphasis on what the young man needed to know, what his spiritual armor was, what made him a complete man, a complete farmer, cobbler or apprentice, all on the premise of his responsibility to the culture and his personal incapacity if he failed to meet the requirements of manhood and faith. But the approach now is radically different. Parents are deluged with information about the treatment of this new-born messiah, the hope of the future, and his needs. They are told what parents must know about the needs of their children, and the incalculable harm that can be wrought by ignorant if well-meaning parents. The needs are made very specific in a variety of books, on for example, the child from three to five, the children from five to ten, and so on. To have a child now is no longer an act of nature but a matter of painful research. "Essential" education is in terms of the needs of the child, not in terms of the requirements of God and society. The consequences, of course, are children who are group-directed and consumption-centered, whose attitude toward life is one of appetite rather than responsibility.[3]

The implications of such education are far-reaching. When the needs of the child are central, and a moral neutrality is asserted with regard to the new-born babe, then the basic responsibility and fault is the state's and society's, and corrective action is not personal action but social and statist action. It is not man who needs changing as much as society. Thus the persistent hope is

[3] The child is well aware of this orientation. From the author's own experience in a church vacation school, he saw a child who had, over a period of years, abused every teacher's insistence that, with a loving attempt to meet the child's needs, he would be won over. Finally, when the patience of one teacher gave way, because of deliberately provocative behavior, to explosive anger, the boy, afraid that punishment was at last to come, cried out, "Don't you hit me! Don't you hit me! What I need is love and affection!"

that a good omelette can be made out of bad eggs, to use an apt adage. The net result is that statism flourishes in such a context.

Again, such education is "for life" and is thus impotent in terms of the realities of life in that life is seen in terms of needs and appetite. As Crabb has pointed out, education was once in terms of life and death alike, the whole of reality, and had, as an element of its discipline, the concept of the omniscience of God. "Thou God seest me" (Gen. 16:13) was set in the context of responsibility and accountability. This world was "a vale of soul-making," and that true discipline "which springs from an inner conviction" the goal of education. Chastening was an act of grace on God's part and a manifestation of care and government on the part of parents and school.[4] That this chastening was faulty, and itself affected by the old Adam in the chastener at times, goes without saying, but that it was indeed a manifestation of love and concern is equally certain. And, while there is much in modern studies of children which is of value, the basic orientation cannot be accepted. The background of its thinking can be understood by studying a work very influential in its day and frequently reprinted, written in 1904 by Horne, assistant professor of Philosophy and Pedagogy at Dartmouth. According to Horne the goal of all history, evolution and education is this: "the individual is *not* the universal but it will be."[5] Since Horne's day, the orientation has become less philosophical but none the less centered on the individual and more and more in terms of needs. If international politics have required a re-thinking of education, it has only been to shift the concept of needs from the individual to the state. Scientists are needed and engineers. The responsibility and discipline required are in terms of state needs, not in terms of God and creation in His image. As a result, *while curriculum content may improve, educational goals have been further diminished.* The religion of statism cannot create re-

[4] Crabb, *op. cit.,* pp. 32, 114 f.
[5] Herman Harrell Horne. *The Philosophy of Education,* p. 286, New York: Macmillan, 1908.

sponsible people; it can only compel responsibility, ending thereby in the very externalism against which Dewey and his followers revolted so strongly. But externalism is the only resort, other than collapse, if we reject that Christian orthodoxy which is productive of responsibility. Education has thus become statist by default, having no other alternative to Christianity. According to Lazarsfeld and Thielens, themselves statist in sympathies, in those colleges they, on their standards, rate as high in quality, 58% of the social scientists are "permissive," that is statist in their faith, and another 30% somewhat so, and only 12% conservative. In the colleges rated medium high, 44% are statist, 33% "somewhat permissive," and 23% conservative. The medium low colleges are 27% permissive, 24% somewhat permissive, 49% conservative, and the "low" quality colleges are low with 'only' 22% permissive, 19% somewhat permissive, and 59% conservative.[6] If these figures are to be believed, we have the sorry spectacle of a very large percentage of all social scientists dedicated to the statist concept which is today rapidly destroying all liberty and prostituting all knowledge.

Apart from the implicit contempt of liberty and learning, another fact appears in this report, the use of the word "permissive" as equivalent to a belief in statism, socialism, and welfare planning. At first glance, it seems to be a monstrous presumption, and some reviewers have spoken bluntly of this as evasive and prejudicial terminology. There may no doubt be an element of this present, but, more than that, it reflects a very definite background of educational faith and language of the school of Dewey. Dewey, reflecting the developed faith of the Enlightenment and of Froebel, in enunciating in 1900 the three premises of education, began the association of permissiveness and statism. Two of the three premises declared the primary business of education to be training in group or cooperative living, in a statist society

---

[6] Paul F. Lazarsfeld and Wagner Thielens, Jr., with a field report by David Riesman: *The Academic Mind, Social Scientists in a Time of Crisis*, p. 162. Glencoe, Ill.: The Free Press, 1958.

seen religiously by Dewey as the true Kingdom of God. A third
premise declared "that the primary root of all educational activity is in the instinctive, impulsive attitudes and activities of
the child, and not in the presentation and application of external
material."[7] Dewey also stated, "The conduct of the pupil should
be governed by himself according to the social needs of his community, rather than by arbitrary laws."[8] Permissiveness and
statism are essentially related. The assumption of responsibility
by the state inevitably involves the surrender of responsibility
by the individual to the group and the state. Every period of
social decline and of statism sees also the rise in popularity of
the concept of permissiveness. It becomes a basic need of "free"
man, now seen as free only in terms of emancipation from work
and responsibility. Statism is liberty and permissiveness to the
man in full flight from the responsibilities of manhood, in rebellion against the requirements of God, and with an immature love
of play rather than work. "The glorious liberty of the sons of
God" is to them an unspeakable bondage. The concept of the
child in terms of needs and moral neutrality inevitably means a
radical re-interpretation of the concept of liberty. Educationally,
the child considered in terms of needs must be given automatic
promotions to prevent any sense of inferiority, frustration or mal-
adjustment. Socially, the same child must be guaranteed cradle to
grave security lest a psychic trauma be produced. The cure for
failure to learn is to devaluate learning, and the cure for social
failure is to devaluate success. Inevitably, the only teachers who
succeed in terms of such schools are those who share in the basic
premises, or supinely permit their propagation with the result that,
despite the academic degrees, the teachers are less and less teachers and more and more propagandists of the statist creed. Their
obvious inferiority has been substantially demonstrated by the
army's draft deferment testing program, which reveals that not

[7] John Dewey, "Froebel's Educational Principles," *The Elementary School
Record*, p. 143, Vol. I, no. 5, June, 1900.

[8] John Dewey, Article I, "The Principles of Progressive Education," *Progressive Education*, p. vi, Vol. I, no. 1, April, 1924.

only are prospective teachers the lowest in intelligence and ability of any group, and by a substantial margin, but that those who are headed for school administration are a radically inferior group. As Whyte comments, on analyzing the figures, "It is now well evident that a large proportion of the younger people who will one day be in charge of our secondary-school system are precisely those with the least aptitude for education of all Americans attending college."[9] Educators are unwilling to admit these facts, and, when forced to, plead that low pay drives away the better prospects.[10] But the falsity of this claim is apparent when it is realized that the same applies to systems with high pay, and the fact that *administrators, usually well paid, represent the lowest calibre of all.* Money then is not the issue, because at least administration would draw men of intellectual ability and aptitude. The fact is that statist education, resting as it does on a philosophy repugnant to free and responsible men, does not and cannot draw a high level of men. Christian schools, often paying less, are nonetheless able to draw dedicated men and culturally literate men, this in spite of handicaps a young and developing concept in education faces. C. S. Lewis has commented on the educational situation aptly, calling attention to the "tragi-comedy of our situation —we continue to clamour for those very qualities we are rendering impossible . . . In a sort of ghastly simplicity we remove the organs and demand the function. We make men without chests and expect of them virtue and enterprise. We laugh at honour and are shocked to find traitors in our midst. We castrate and bid the geldings be fruitful."[11]

As long as education is statist, the concept of the child and of

---

[9] William H. Whyte Jr.: *The Organization Man*, p. 83 f. New York: Simon and Schuster, 1956.

[10] For a factual analysis of the wealth in tax funds going to education, see Roger A. Freeman: *School Needs in the Decade Ahead.* Washington: The Institute for Social Science Research, 1958. Education, rather than starved, is surpassed only by national defense in expenditures.

[11] C. S. Lewis: *The Abolition of Man*, or Reflections on Education with special reference to the teaching of English in the upper forms of schools, p. 16. New York: Macmillan, 1947.

man will be statist. We shall be busy castrating and bidding the geldings be fruitful. It is not enough to maintain private and Christian schools in the midst of a statist culture. The two are ultimately exclusive. In 1922, the state of Oregon attempted to make all education statist, being stopped only by a Supreme Court still dedicated to older concepts. But, as Clark has stated, "under any government the Christian principle is plain: Render unto Caesar the things which are Caesar's, and unto God the things that are God's. Children do not belong to Caesar."[12] The Christian cannot rest content with extracting an indulgence for himself; he must attack the fundamental statist concept, separating all education, including parochial, private, and Christian schools, as well as "public" schools, from the state and from state financial aid in any form. Statist education is ultimately the annihilation of man as man. To the statist, the thought of the withdrawal of any area from the grasp of government smacks of anarchism, the dark ages and total collapse. To attack statist education is to be villified as an enemy of education. Even the critics of contemporary education who are statist in their premises are subjected to a vindictive and irrational attack. But the unavoidable issue remains: statist education is the bulwark of this statist concept of life, enabling it to mold the child to its faith and to obliterate every form of non-statist culture. There can be no attack on statism without a like attack on statist education. Education must be truly free. The churches have not perished by being cut off from state funds in various countries. Rather, they have thrived and are gaining a new vitality and relevancy. In like manner, the "Dis-establishment" of the schools will be productive of true scholarship and vital education.

[12] Gordon H. Clark: *A Christian Philosophy of Education*, p. 195 f. Grand Rapids: Eerdmans, 1946.

7

The Bible in the Christian School

The teaching of the Bible in the Christian school as its basic religious and cultural premise, can be wholly or partially neutralized if certain non-biblical presuppositions govern the teaching. The Bible indeed has often been an alien book in the church precisely because so many presuppositions in the churchman place a standing barrier between himself and the Scriptures.

Again, it is possible to be drawn to biblical data with alien presuppositions in mind. Van Til has excellently illustrated this in *Paul at Athens*. The philosophers were at first drawn to Paul's statements concerning the resurrection of Jesus Christ. They saw it in the context of their philosophy, a world of ultimate chance yet capable of revealing strange and new potentialities. Perhaps this report of a resurrection at Jerusalem indicated a new potentiality of and the next development in man. Heard, however, in the context of the eternal decree, the sovereign God, and Christ the judge of all men, this same data was suddenly hopelessly uninteresting. To the Stoics and Epicureans who heard Paul, this doctrine was hostile to the basic egocentricity of their philoso-

phies, and their concept of the autonomy of man. For them God
had to be the unknown or unknowable. Accordingly, they could
not hear a God so clearly known and so definitely sovereign.
Hellenic and modern philosophical presuppositions all too often
color man's approach to Scripture.

But this is not all. One of the most prevalent of presuppositions
in biblical teaching is *moralism,* which reduces biblical faith from
religious to *moralistic* dimensions. This is especially prevalent in
the teaching of children.[1] The non-Christian is incurably moralistic, and his insistence on viewing life moralistically gives the
Christian an illusory and dangerous "common ground." But
Christianity is fundamentally anti-moralistic (but not anti-moral,
of course) and this constituted Paul's offense, in that he pointed
up this contrast. For Scripture, the godly man is the *saved* man,
not the self-consciously *good* man. It is not a contrast between
moral and immoral but between godly and ungodly, holy and
wicked, and the moral man, as witness the Pharisees, can epito-
mize ungodliness. Yet the moralistic construction creeps into
Christian thinking. Even so fine a book as Vos' *Child's Story
Bible,* and it is without equal, has an occasional trace of this.

> The demons hate everything that is good. Most of all they hate
> God. And they do not want us to love Him, or to be good, and
> go to live with Him in Heaven after we die.[2]

But if goodness is a matter of hatred and fear of hell, it can only
be because it is a threat to hell's existence and a means to God,
hardly a Christian doctrine. Not goodness in itself, but holiness is
the issue, that righteousness which is by faith in Jesus Christ.
Satan is not concerned with our *moral* wickedness but our *spiritual* wickedness. This is the biblical concept. The summons is, Be
ye holy, for I am holy. Our righteousness and morality are not for
our sakes, or for our satisfaction in virtue, but for the Lord's sake
and His ends, and our fellowship with Him. Thus, without antino-

[1] See the appendix on "The Menace of the Sunday School."
[2] Catherine F. Vos: *The Child's Story Bible,* p. 28. Grand Rapids: Eerdmans,
1952.

mianism, Scripture sees the sins of the saints from this *religious* rather than *moralistic* perspective. Notice Shimei's denunciation of David as a bloody man (II Sam. 16:7), for which Shimei stood self-condemned, but God, in so different a context and in fundamental love toward and respect for David, expressed a similar opinion (I Chron. 28:3).

Perhaps no better instance of this basic problem can be cited than the story of Rahab (Joshua 2). The evasiveness with which many theologians handle this narrative testifies to the moralism of their faith. Rahab had a choice to make: 1) she could tell the truth and surrender the spies, two godly men, to death. 2) she could lie and save their lives. This is the kind of situation the moralist hates and refuses to accept. Either course involves some evil, however the moralist seeks to deny it. The question is, which is the lesser of two evils? Our choices are rarely black and white ones; we rarely have the luxury of an absolute choice. But we do have the continual opportunity to make decisions in terms of an absolute faith, however gray the immediate situation. This faith Rahab had. Whether she lied or not was relatively unimportant as compared to the lives of two godly men. She lied and saved their lives. For this, James singled her out, together with Abraham, as an instance of vital faith, of faith which was not mere opinion but a matter of life and action (James 2:25). Again, Hebrews 11:31 singled this same act as an instance of true faith. It is useless evasion to try to abstract something from the act as praiseworthy while condemning her for the lie, and a violation of the unity of life. Rahab clearly lied, but her lie represented a moral choice as against sending two godly men to death, and for this she became an ancestress of Jesus Christ (Matt. 1:5). For the moralist, it is important that he stand in his own self-righteousness, and Rahab's alternative is intolerable, because it makes some kind of sin inescapable at times. For the godly man, who stands, not in his own righteousness but the righteousness of Christ, his own purity is not the essence of the matter but that God's will be done. And God, in this situation, certainly willed that the lives of the spies be saved, not that the individual come forth able to say, I never tell a lie.

But, we are told by the moralist, if Rahab had told the truth, God would have been bound to honor her integrity and to deliver her and the spies, and Rahab had an obligation to tell the truth irrespective of the consequences. Several fallacies, characteristic of moralism, are involved here:

1. Moral choice, it is held, involves a simple, uncomplicated, rational issue.
2. It is always a choice between absolute right and wrong.
3. The central issue is always the preservation of the individual's moral purity rather than a transcendent factor.
4. Poetic justice is always operative; virtue is always rescued and rewarded, and truth always triumphant.

But this is not biblical Christianity, but 18th century Deism with a strong dash of Spenser's *Faerie Queene!* Paul could say, echoing the Psalmist (Ps. 44:22) "For thy sake we are killed all the day long; we are accounted as sheep for the slaughter" (Rom. 8:26). That Scripture affirms an ultimate triumph of the *godly* (as differentiated from the *moral*) is beyond question, but it does not affirm the concept of poetic justice. We cannot allow so radical a falsification of the faith to be projected onto Scripture.

The doctrine of poetic justice in effect requires a rewriting of Scripture, history and literature. An instance of the latter is Nahum Tate's revision of *King Lear,* about 1680, which was then the acting version until 1823, about 150 years. Tate had Lear triumphant, and, in Edgar's concluding words affirmed the successfulness of "Truth and Virtue." He felt it morally necessary to make "the Tale conclude in a Success to the innocent distrest Persons" and give poetic justice full sway.

Jesus answered an early version of the same concept plainly and bluntly:

> There were present at that season some that told him of the Galileans, whose blood Pilate had mingled with their sacrifices.

And Jesus answering said unto them, Suppose ye that these Galileans were sinners above all the Galileans, because they suffered such things? I tell you, Nay: but, except ye repent, ye shall all likewise perish. Or those eighteen, upon whom the tower of Siloam fell, and slew them, think ye that they were sinners above all men that dwelt in Jerusalem? I tell you, Nay: but, except ye repent, ye shall all likewise perish (Luke 13:1-5).

The Book of Job is again an answer to a similar demand for poetic justice, which is patently anti-biblical.

Again, we cannot allow teachers or students to project modern secularism onto the Bible. Religious secularism involves a schizophrenic division of life, so that only a limited area is reserved for religious activity. The basic unity of life is broken. As anyone who has been a missionary can testify, unsophisticated pagans are unable to understand the radical division in the Western Christian's life between "religion" and "life", between the sacred and the secular. To accept the modern world-view as normal and then attempt to understand biblical law and the prophetic burden, for example, is an impossibility.

Furthermore, it is necessary to know biblical faith and doctrine, and its basic presuppositions. If God be not truly God in our philosophy and thinking, then man ceases to be man, and reality disappears into a nebulous relativity. Facts do not exist in themselves, as though they were self-created and self-existent, but they exist because created and sustained by the will of God and have no meaning apart from Him who is the starting point of all knowledge. In affirming this, we do not say that the Bible is to be used as a source book in biology or to replace a paleontological study in Africa. As Van Til has stated it, "The Bible does not claim to offer a rival theory that may or may not be true. It claims to have the truth about all facts."[3] Thus, it is not claimed that one should go to the Scriptures instead of Africa. Rather, it is claimed that no fact can be truly known, nor its existence even

[3] C. Van Til: *Metaphysics of Apologetics*, p. 114, 1931.

posited, without the light of Scripture, without the God of the Bible and the revelation therein given.

Another point is fundamental. The Bible must be taught in terms of its claimed ramifications, which are far-reaching. The law, for example, is *particular* and *principial*. Scripture gives us examples of this, as witness the law regarding the muzzling of the ox, Deuteronomy 25:4, I Corinthians 9:9f., I Timothy 5:18:

1. A humane treatment of the ox is called for. The ox deserves a portion of the grain he has helped tread out. By this elementary statement, true and necessary, a broader principle is asserted. If the ox must be rewarded, how much more so man?

2. Thus it follows that, "He that ploweth ought to plow in hope, and he that thresheth to thresh in hope of partaking" (1 Cor. 9:10 RV). A principle is asserted with regard to labor in general and the ministry in particular.

3. Accordingly, "The laborer is worthy of his hire" (I Tim. 5:18).

4. Thus a principle regarding labor and remuneration is definitely asserted and made all the more binding because it is even applicable in terms of animal labor, i.e., on a sub-human level.

Another instance of such usage is Ecclesiastes 10:8, "Whoso breaketh through a fence (hedge) a serpent shall bite him." Here was a matter of observation; hedges were the usual places for serpents, and to break through a boundary hedge was to run very heavy risk of snake-bite. Thus, to break a hedge-fence was to bring unexpected judgment on oneself. Man, by breaking the fence of law around the tree in Eden, brought the Serpent and death upon himself. Life is strictly circumscribed by God's law. Never for a moment can we escape from the workings of His immutable decrees. Every hedge or wall has its serpent.[4]

Again, it must be realized that biblical faith and doctrine are never abstractions. Invaluable as creeds and catechisms are,

[4] See G. H. Lang: *The Parabolic Teaching of Scripture*, p. 11f. Grand Rapids: Eerdmans, 1955.

it must always be remembered that the Bible never gives us an abstraction but an account of life, an incarnation of doctrine, so to speak. It defines faith, for example, in terms of what is believed in specific situations, and in terms of the lives of men. Abraham believed God, said Amen to God, and it was reckoned unto him for righteousness; it was faith in the living God in terms of the trying context of life, not an abstract assent to a theoretical concept. Invaluable as all formularies are, they have value only as they point us to the text of Scripture and an understanding of it. Thus, ultimately, the Bible in the school must stand as in the church as its own interpreter: "The infallible rule of interpretation of Scripture is the Scripture itself."

8

The Mysticism of the Public Schools

Two of the cardinal aspects of the modern concept of education are, as it has been pointed out, first, that it is productive of
intellectual schizophrenia, and, second, that it is a continuation
and secular manifestation of the medieval concept of society.

It should be noted that schizophrenia is an especially prevalent
psychosis in this era, constituting a large portion of the mental
sicknesses under treatment. Schizophrenia has been called by
some the greatest disease menace of our time, and its affinities to
our culture are especially deep. For this reason, it is even in
serious cases often and in milder forms constantly, not readily
noticed by the general population. It is a radical split between
thought and *feeling,* is productive of phantasy rather than action,
involves a withdrawal from reality, (as witness culturally the
withdrawal of modern philosphers of the logico-analytic school)
and is often characterized also by a studied rebellion against
mental health. Strecker has quoted, with disagreement, the
"gloomy remark" of "an able psychiatrist," "I never knew a
schizophrenic patient who could not get well, and yet I never

knew one who did."[1] This observation has some merit, in that it catches the negative orientation of schizophrenia; *it has as studied a love of unity in phantasy as it has a rejection of unity in reality*. This is especially characteristic of the cultural schizophrenia of our day, with its world-embracing phantasies of unity combined with the reality of disunity, not only within the society and the family, but also within the very mind of man.

The secularized medievalism of education is an aspect of this sickness. Medieval cartographers, in drawing maps, placed Jerusalem in the center and made the map circular, thus making it the hub, pivot and heart of all humanity. Brought up to date, the ideal was that the whole of Europe, and, in effect, the known and contingent world, were to be made one city, the true Jerusalem made visible. Otto I, in re-establishing the Roman Empire in terms of this concept, is represented as the bearer of this concept on a liturgical vessel with the inscription "Jerusalem visio pacis." All society was to be an incarnation of a universal and supernatural reality; hence unity was the basic premise whether under the Empire or under the Church. The question, as it developed, was as to the institutional manifestation and control of that order.

The Protestant Reformers began their work under the influence of that same concept but rapidly gave priority to *truth* above *unity* and as the only true ground of unity. Truth being divisive, society rapidly became pluralistic.

The Enlightenment, however, had its own version of the medieval faith, and its own conception of the heavenly city, a dream no less evident in Karl Marx, in the champions of world democracy, and in the one-world state idea. The modern concept of education is an affirmation of this faith, and, for all its protestations, is anti-pluralistic and believes in a secular Jerusalem whose priests are educators. A 'public' school education is deemed culturally necessary in order that the child might participate in the ethos of that order and become one with it. In essence, the

[1] Edward A. Strecker: *Basic Psychiatry,* p. 210. New York: Random House, 1952.

contemporary goal of education is mysticism, secular and naturalistic but nonetheless mysticism. God, Tao and Brahma have been replaced by the mystical group, and the purpose of education is to develop group experience and sensitivity. We are told that conservatives, being "largely uninformed as to the real objectives of education in a democracy," considers the "essentials" to be "frills," while the "non-essentials" in the curriculum, having "the weight of tradition behind them," are defended whereas they are the true frills. They do not see that " 'the Letter killeth, but the Spirit giveth life.' Vigilance must be constantly employed to guard against the devastating impact of the printed word upon independent thought."[2] To be educated means, not learning, but unswerving loyalty to democratic ideals as the school defines them. "The entire curriculum, the entire life of the school, in fact, should be a youthful experience in democratic living, quickening social inventiveness and agitating the social conscience. So are citizens for the democratic state successfully educated."[3] Nothing could be plainer. The goal of education is not learning but experience; hence the 'inadequacy' and 'failure' of 'private' and parochial schools, which both emphasize learning and, (as a by-product) give an alien experience. Learning, indeed, has its place in this concept, and can be heavily emphasized as occasions of state may require, but basic to the learning is the mystical devotion to the new god, the state, whose high priest is the state school. That new god is sometimes seen with a communist face, then again with a democratic countenance, but the mysticisms each invoke are but variations of a common heresy, and secular revivals of clearly medieval concepts.

But man, being at war with himself, cannot, for all his phantasies, turn his dream of unity into reality. The more zealously he pursues the phantasy, the more radical will his collapse become. His pursuit of the experience is a love of death (Prov. 8:36) and has as its harbinger acute and chronic anxiety. And,

---

[2] *The Purposes of Education in American Democracy,* pp. 145, 149.
[3] *Ibid.,* p. 123.

because of his schizophrenic dissociation, his anxiety is no warning of present danger but a phantom born of flight. But not even in space and its generous time can man ever hope to escape from himself and the issues of his own being.

The development of this mysticism is old in its roots, having certain inheritances from the Renaissance and the Enlightenment, in their exaltation of man, but its more immediate source is Rousseau. Stated in its mildest form, the concept asserted that majority will creates law and grants rights. This majority will constituted the source of true justice and liberty. Anything else was tyranny; any other authority was slavery. Bakunin reduced the idea to its logical conclusions and asserted two things: first, "If there is a God, man is a slave." Second, "liberty is a denial of all authority, and God is authority." Paul had declared, "Where the Spirit of the Lord is, there is liberty" (II Cor. 3:17); now the reverse was held to be true: where the spirit of man is, there is liberty. Politics and education addressed themselves to communion and communication with that spirit. But, as Le Bon observed of his day, "the masses have never thirsted after truth." "It is not the need of liberty but of servitude that is always predominant in the soul of the crowd. They are so bent on obedience that they instinctively submit to whoever declares himself their master."[4]

The creation of mass man and the development of the concept of the general will have had inevitable effects on man. First, responsibility has been transferred from the individual to the group, now the supreme authority. Second, social pressure is accentuated wherever the group reigns. ("The fear of man bringeth a snare: but whoso putteth his trust in the LORD, shall be safe," Prov. 29:25). No tyrant is as omnipresent and dangerous as man, or more fearfully and abjectly served. Third, it destroys responsibility on higher levels also, in that, unlike delegation of power in a republic and government in terms of a higher law, it

[4] Gustave Le Bon: *The Crowd, A Study of the Popular Mind*, pp. 110, 121. London: Benn, 1896, 1932.

involves rather a bare representation of the people, now the source of law. Fourth, it results in mysticism, and the language of politics, education and theology has become experience, participation, correspondence, integration, and the like. Even the familiar expression "college education" is giving way, in educational terminology to "college experience," and the goal of this experience is "how to live democratically."[5] Fraternities are attacked, not on the ground of their possible relationship to poor learning, but in terms of this same mystical concept.

Mysticism strives for union and absorption into the divine whole. This union is the highest goal of life, surpassing by far any other concern. And, because it is held that there is a common substance in the individual and the divine whole, not salvation but self-realization is the means to the religious goal, and self-realization is essentially the disappearance of the self into the divine whole. Subject and object, god and man, humanity and the individual, are fused and merged into an undivided *one*. The mystical experience begins with ecstacy but must culminate in anaesthesia. Before this is accomplished, the process of absorption ostensibly invades the individual with the energies and experiences of the divine whole. The insulation and privacy of individuality give way to an all-inclusive unity and an experience in which oneness becomes the highest value.

By a slight alteration and modernization of terminology, this description of mysticism can be altered into a description of contemporary educational goals and the concept of the educational experience in democratic living.

The success of such statist and mystical educational theory, Le Bon, in a more practical context, long ago noted. Statist education in France, in the latter part of the 19th century, created a generation that avoided work in free enterprises in favor of government positions, (creating the immense civil service that is now France's surest government and greatest handicap). The

---

[5] R. Freeman Butts: *A Cultural History of Western Education, Its Social and Intellectual Foundations*, p. 584. New York: McGraw-Hill, 1955.

educational preparation was not in terms of self-direction and independent action, but in terms of state functions and with "a superstitious confidence in the State, whom it regards as a sort of Providence."[6] The result was, practically, a growing correlation, in view of this kind of instruction, between the increase of such education and criminality. Le Bon could accuse this educational theory with transforming "the majority of those who have undergone it into enemies of society."[7] This is to simplify unduly the problem; as we have seen, the religious presuppositions of modern man which underlie both pupil and school make both culpable and both victims alike of a deadly faith.

This mysticism sees its god as beyond law: the individual can go bankrupt, but the state will always have an answer that will over-ride the old economic realities. Hence, more power to the state. Problems become difficult for the individual, but the state has a higher wisdom whereby it can deal with all situations. If the state falters or fails, it is only because the wrong combinations of men guide it, and a reshuffling is believed to be the answer to the problem, not any question as to the inadequacy of statism. Medieval man never revealed so intense and zealous a faith as does modern man in his devotion to the cult of the state.

Because the modern concept of education is a religious faith, it will increasingly be hostile to all non-statist forms of education in that they separate the individual from the ineffable experience it alone can give. Thus an increasingly bitter struggle will be waged against all "enemies," to use an N.E.A. term, of the public school. In terms of this, the Christian and other 'private' schools will be hopelessly inadequate if they see the issue as merely their survival or freedom. It is a 'holy' or religious war that is waged against them and the issue can only be resolved as a revitalized orthodox Christianity faces the implications of its faith and develops them consistently in terms of the whole of life. This cannot be done in terms of a new medievalism or any nostalgia for past

---

[6] Le Bon, *op. cit.*, p. 93.
[7] *Ibid.*, p. 91.

forms, nor by an evasion of the fact of epistemological pluralism, for such an unrealistic attitude leads to attempts to recreate the past instead of recognizing the realities of the present. On the other hand, there can be no retreat into a permanent remnant concept, because the biblical concept of the Kingdom forbids it. Moreover, the transcendental unity of God's Kingdom is such that it includes even the wrath of man, and makes all things serve His sovereign and omnipotent purpose. Whether with man's will, or against it, all man's cultural activity will contribute to the unified structure of the Kingdom. In terms of the realities of the development of epistemological self-consciousness, the Christian has every ground for confidence concerning the future.

But confidence must be the ground, not of sloth, but of action, for the attack is mounting, and the demand increasing that all American youth be in 'public' or statist schools, such an assertion coming from none less than James B. Conant. Ganse Little, president of the Board of Christian Education of the United Presbyterian Church U.S.A., has called parochial education "a kind of brainwashing" and defended 'public' schools as the means of true education, apparently confident that state schools have an objectivity and that their secular faith involves no indoctrination. More than that, the 1925 Oregon Case decision is now being questioned. The Supreme Court then ruled, "The fundamental theory of liberty upon which all governments in the Union repose excludes any general power of the state to standardize its children by forcing them to accept instruction from public teachers only." But John L. Childs, professor emeritus at Columbia's Teachers College, has questioned the right of non-statist schools to operate freely, stating, "Unless church educational practices which are assumed to have been sanctioned by that historic decision of the Supreme Court are reviewed and revised, the future of the common school is not one of promise."[8] Thus, even as discipline col-

[8] Cited from *The Educational Forum*, January, 1955, by Walter A. De Jong, in "Do Christian Schools Brainwash?", p. 8, *Torch and Trumpet*, VII, 4, September, 1957.

lapses and hoodlumism increases as a constant problem, the statist educators grow more vocal in their demands that all youth be subjected to the mystical experience of which they are the high priests. The state needs, they believe, to standardize "its children."

9

The Future of the Christian School

Culture is, as Henry R. Van Til has pointed out in *The Calvin-istic Concept of Culture*,[1] "religion externalized." The future of the Christian school is closely linked, as a result, with certain cultural and historical facts. If Christianity has lost the ability to create and maintain a culture, then the Christian school has a peripheral and dying function today, but if Christianity's cultural power remains yet to be manifested, then the Christian school has an essential and as yet unrealized role to play.

Scripture gives us certain principles of cultural expectations. According to Hebrews 12:18-29, history, from the giving of the law at Sinai to the coming of Christ, was subjected to a great shaking, to be followed by a second (Heb. 12:18-29, Matt. 24), from the fall of Jerusalem to the end of the world. The prophets addressed themselves to the implications of that first shaking, and the 'major' prophets give us the roll-call of the judgment of the nations in preparation for the advent of the messianic ruler and his Kingdom. The purpose of this first shaking was to prepare the world for his coming, while the second shaking will destroy

[1] Presbyterian and Reformed Publishing Co., 1959.

all false faiths and refuges and make plain the implications of his coming, so that the things which alone cannot be shaken might remain. The Book of Revelation is also addressed to this same question. Man will be allowed no false security, no hiding place, no paradise apart from God, and the relentless course of history is the destruction of all such attempts and the growing futility of flight or escape.

The same subject is the concern of Matthew 13:24-30, the tares and wheat parable which declares that the difference between the Kingdom of God and the kingdom of darkness will become progressively more apparent. History is thus a process of epistemological self-consciousness and separation. The tares and wheat will grow side by side at the beginning, largely indistinguishable. Tares or darnel are psuedo-wheat, whose difference from wheat becomes manifest as maturity comes. As cultures come to maturity, they come to epistemological self-consciousness, and as world history develops, and as a totality matures, the same process of maturation and self-consciousness will manifest itself. Eschatology thus does not speak of an end that simply appears without causal connection to history but as a culminating act to a process of culmination. To look backward culturally, therefore, to the time of undifferentiation, is to resist the movement of history. Indeed, in times of cultural undifferentiation, "everybody goes to church," and the church often has simpler internal problems, but only because the tare has not recognizably and self-consciously become a tare, and the wheat has only a mild awareness of the demands and implications of his nature and position. The process of self-consciousness therefore involves a radical break-down of the true church outwardly as a prelude to its realization of its strength and position realistically. Thus, while the Christian, as a participant in the events, can share in the common dismay at the tragedies and mounting crises of history, he must nevertheless welcome these crises as the necessary and God-ordained shaking of history. Even more than Augustine, he must recognize that the fall of his Rome is a necessary step toward the establishment of the Kingdom of God.

But the process of maturation and self-consciousness is two-fold. The natural man, as he moves ahead in terms of an epistemological self-consciousness and awareness, steadily drops that form of conformity to godliness, purpose, meaning, and social cohesion which once marked his life. There is progressively operative a radical disintegration of the natural man. The more obviously he becomes a tare, the more obviously he surrenders the appearance that made him earlier seemingly a part of the wheat field. There is therefore in each maturing culture, and in the totality of history as it matures, a progressive degeneration of the natural man, a process of self consciousness which makes the forms of conformity more and more irrelevant and absurd. The description of Romans I becomes progressively more and more applicable. Meanwhile, the wheat must mature as wheat.

In particular cultures, the process of self-consciousness can be readily pin-pointed. Is it beginning to manifest itself in history as a whole? Is it present in some tentative and embryonic fashion in our own day? Are the elements of community in radical disintegration, not merely in particular cultures, but in all cultures? Is the cultural crisis thus a world-wide one?

To answer this question, let us first analyze a few aspects of the common life which are now in process of erosion. The further back we go in history the more strongly we are impressed by the strong sense of *community* that once prevailed. However grim certain relationships were, a strong sense of human community characterized man. This can be extensively documented, but perhaps never so beautifully as from Genesis 18. We find therein the ancient concept of hospitality clearly portrayed. Abraham, seated under the oaks of Mamre during the heat of the day, saw three strangers approaching. The identity of the strangers was unknown to him, but the fact that travel-weary strangers approached made immediate demands on Abraham. Any offense against hospitality was an unspeakable crime, of which only the most depraved were capable (Gen. 19:1-9, Judges 19-20). Accordingly Abraham immediately went forward and in greeting said, "My Lord, if now I have found favor in thy sight, pass not away from thy servant," and offered shelter and food. Granted that this greeting represented a formal and ritual approach, it was still indicative of the fact that hospitality was both a responsibility or requirement as well as a privilege. A stranger, if not an enemy to be killed, was a brother to be received. This same concept prevailed very strongly among Arabs, despite their cultural decline, until the past century but is now in rapid erosion. Archeologists in Palestine found it necessary to eat salt, that is, share a common meal with the local sheik, as a kind of incorporation into his people. Every meal involved an affirmation of community and an act of incorporation of which the Sacrament of the Last Supper is a ritual reminder. Originally, it was the common meal of the Christian people or race as contrasted to the table of demons. Among the older generation of Paiutes and Shoshones in Nevada, people who have of late rapidly passed on, the same concept of community was apparent. Other Indians could come to the Western Shoshone Reservation confident of a welcome and a place to stay, even to remain for lengthy months. No matter how crowded and limited the host's facilities, a one-room cabin and a host of children, the stranger was made welcome. Orphans similarly had no problem: they moved in to another family at will. By contrast, the white man was a cold and inhospitable monster, and Christians peculiar people who talked about love and welcomed no one. The law of hospitality had certain presuppositions common to men, and certain obligations binding on host and guest. Today these things have become impossibilities. What men could once expect of strangers, they can no longer expect of their own children, or dare ask for. The sense of community is rapidly disappearing, and even those rural areas which were once the strongholds of such solidarity now see its erosion. In virtually every part of the world, the sense of community is giving way to the erosive forces of modern life and the over-riding control of the state. Society is giving way to the state, and communities exist now only as created and developed by minorities against the current. But there can be no return to the old solidarity. Mankind's epistemological self-consciousness is divisive of such unity, and, on the part of the unregenerate, increasingly hostile to such private communication and interdependence.

Another area now subject to rapid erosion is the *family*. The centrality of the family in biblical culture is clear-cut. The two most serious crimes were offenses against God and offenses against the family. In many cultures, the most fearful crime of all was parricide, an offense that rendered the guilty hateful even to himself. A man without a family was a contradiction, an object of distrust and suspicion. The family undergirded every aspect of a man's life, and, in Scripture, the very concept of salvation was in terms of a kinsman-redeemer. The authority of the family was strong and fundamental, not an oppressive power but a supporting authority. The family today, however, in all its varieties, is subject to rapid disintegration everywhere and only the modern atomistic and eroded family survives in many areas. The polyandrous family of Tibet is now being subjected to the disintegrating power of communism, and the old family system of China has been forcibly broken up. In Africa, tribe and family alike are surrendering to Western corrosion, and the handwriting is on the wall for the Eskimos no less than the jungle folk of the world. Outside of the world of Jesus Christ, the family is steadily breaking down. Family culture is in a rapid process of deterioration everywhere, and as man's crisis is stepped up and the shaking of the nations increases, the old forms of life disappear more rapidly. And there is no return to the past. In the past, as with the fall of Rome, familist culture re-appeared, because the collapse did not carry all peoples in the Empire with it. Moreover, in social catalysis today there is no agent that itself remains stable while witnessing or precipitating change. The family in particular is no longer a bystander but itself one of the first subjects of social change. And the family itself, outside limited areas, has abdicated its authority in favor of state and school and become a peripheral institution. Psychiatrists and sociologists, in attempting to revive family culture, emphasize its psychic significance in the development of the child and the emotional health of the adult, and rightly so. But this is to stress one value alone of the home. Its ancient religious, educational, economic, and social centrality is not considered, nor its recall desired. At best, the family is given a limited scope in terms of the future.

The sense of *function and calling* is another area of erosion. Only a broken and dying culture fails to manifest in its members a strong sense of calling. This is today conspicuous by its absence. No 'primitive' culture has been found in which this sense of calling is absent. It was once held that the aboriginal women of Australia, believed to represent the 'lowest' known culture, lacked any sense of function or calling. The long study of Phyllis M. Kaberry, *Aboriginal Woman, Sacred and Profane* (1939), clearly depicts the strong sense of sacred function of aboriginal women in Australia. Imbued with a sense of sacred function, they have a dignity together with a deep satisfaction in their work. Here, as elsewhere, it is westernization which destroys the dignity of position and renders every function profane, empty and meaningless. In biblical faith, man has a calling as prophet, priest and king in Christ and a cosmic significance to his office. But modern man lacks calling; he has excellent working conditions but no sense of vocation. As cultures everywhere are secularized, they are emptied of meaning. Since culture is religion externalized, the absence of faith means the debauching of a culture, and its petrifaction or collapse. And petrification, once possible as with China and Japan, is increasingly less possible as the world comes closer to the door of the sleeping culture and more readily threatens its peace. Men who once lived to work now work to play, to seek escape from responsibility and the pursuit of meaning. Thus man is steadily losing everything that makes him man, everything that characterizes him as created in the image of God. What Van Til has called earlier or creation grace is in rapid process of erosion and death. Man is obliterating everything that once made his life significant because he hates signification. As a result, the characteristic temper of modern man is a perpetual state of anxiety, anxiety because his life means nothing, anxiety because he is constantly burdened by the fact that he has no true burden. During World War II, mental health improved as men gained a cheap "cause" by means of the war and at no cost to their desire for an easy conscience, but it was a short-lived and sickly health. It was borrowed and short-term meaning. A meaningless and purposeless people are dangerous, in that they lust after easy causes and cheap meanings. They find in war and hatred easy causes and convenient demons to exorcise.

A vivid picture of the radical irrationality and meaninglessness of modern man has been given by Georges Simenon in his novel *The Man Who Watched the Trains Go By* (1946). Life is a parcel of senseless rules, and the sucker is the man who persists in following them; the course of wisdom is "to be first to break the rules" and in that way be "sure of not being had." Man being purposeless and without calling, when the routine of his life is broken readily surrenders all the moral standards and principles which were part of that routine. "Nobody obeys the laws if he can help it." Kees Popinga, having no fundamental faith, quickly deteriorates into a common criminal. But both his respectability and criminality were each in turn accidental and without conviction; he was pliable to circumstance and incapable of direction. On his arrest, he sought to write an autobiographical excuse entitled "The Truth about the Kees Popinga Case" but found himself unable to write a word, concluding, "Really, there isn't any truth about it, is there, doctor?" This perceptive novel is unhappily all too accurate. Modern man without faith tends to be a wastebasket into which miscellaneous experiences fall without purpose or meaning. As a result, he substitutes *analysis* for *meaning,* in that *dissection more becomes him than direction.* Morton White has aptly called this *The Age of Analysis.* Philosophically, that analysis has involved a radical evasion of any concept of a world-view or a metaphysics. The traditional concerns of philosophy are by-passed, as are the issues of public and private life, the problems of culture, art, and politics, for a childish and idealistic analysis of language.

Meanwhile, in every area the erosion increases, and man's life becomes more and more meaningless as he is stripped of every structure and form of life except the monolithic state. This is to be expected. The biblical philosophy of history is insistent that the natural man's life does not stand still but moves steadily to epistemological self-consciousness and the deterioration and degeneration his awareness involves. Indeed, the true church is summoned to prepare herself for the day of full cultural responsibility, as witness Paul's appeal, I Cor. 6:1, 2: "Dare any of you, having a matter against another, go to law before the unjust, and not before the saints? Do ye not know that the saints shall judge the world? and if this world shall be judged by you, are ye unworthy to judge the smallest matters?" The word *judge* is here used in the Old Testament sense, *"to govern."* The saints are to govern the world ultimately as alone capable of giving direction, meaning, and cultural form to life in its every aspect. In view of this eventuality, the church must prepare herself by her own internal self-government, by a developed capacity to deal with her problems, by the development of her life in every avenue of home, school, and vocation, and by the philosophical development of her faith in terms of all knowledge and science, for the Christian's function as salt-bearer (i.e., preserving force) and governor of the world. As the cultural collapse is accelerated, God alone can become the source of culture and meaning, and the Christian becomes the cultural force and agent. Natural man is destroying family, community, society, everything that makes life livable, destroying the meaning of work, destroying the meaning of function and even destroying meaning as such, in that current theories of semantics imply that meaning in itself is obsolete.

The summons to a sleeping church are clear-cut: "What, know

ye not that the saints are to judge the world?" This is no time for smug pietism and withdrawal; there is no luxury of being raptured out of problems. The kingdoms of this world are to become the Kingdoms of our Lord and of his Christ. Meanwhile, as the crisis develops, men's hearts fail them for fear. If the cultural destiny of man apart from God is degeneration, then the cultural destiny of the true and consistent Christian must be regeneration, and there is no escaping this responsibility. To evade it is to become salt without savour, cast out and to be trodden under foot of men.

We have therefore an imperative need for Christian education, for the development of a Christian university in terms of Christian-theistic epistemological presuppositions. We need to recognize that nothing is more short-sighted and tragic than the limitations of Christianity to ecclesiastical objectives when its responsibility is in terms of the whole of life, and Jesus Christ is presented in Scripture as mediator of a cosmic as well as personal redemption. Man is called to exercise his image mandate in knowledge, righteousness, holiness and dominion, subduing the earth agriculturally, scientifically, culturally, artistically, in every possible way asserting the crown rights of King Jesus in every realm of life, claiming the kingdoms of this world as the Kingdoms of our Lord and his Christ. The standard of Jesus Christ must be erected in every field of life. This is the fundamental task of Christian education, with the recognition of its growing responsibility as present realities are shaken that the unshakeable might alone remain. In terms of all this, the Christian cannot limit his functioning to the institutional church nor become a power manipulator or a placid or stoical bystander. As Henry Van Til has pointed out, culture is not a neutral enterprise. Because Christianity encompasses the totality of life, it must become in its totality the source of culture. "For a people's religion comes to expression in its culture, and Christians can be satisfied with nothing less than a Christian organization of society."[1]

---

[1] Henry R. Van Til: *The Calvinistic Concept of Culture,* p. 245. Philadelphia: Presbyterian and Reformed, 1959.

10

The End of an Age

One does not have to agree with the philosophies of Spengler, Toynbee, or Berdyaev to recognize that we are at the end of an age. Although no age has been without its tensions, crises, torments, and doubts, these factors are healthy and constructive when they stem from the struggle for and pursuit of a goal in terms of an assured faith and a governing hope. They are then spurs to action rather than grounds of indecision. When, however, man has lost his sense of identity, his basic faith, and has turned from a governing hope to wishful thinking, the absence of meaning results in an absence of coherency of action and an incapacity for self-defense. A culture not convinced of its own value is incapable of its own defense. Its energy is replaced by apathy, and its convictions by the torments of self-analysis. As a result of such a collapse, the "millions of Romans were vanquished by scores of thousands of Germans."[1]

It is not necessary to agree with the faith of a past age in order to recognize its achievements; the important aspects of medieval-

[1] William Carroll Bark: *Origins of the Medieval World*, p. 184. Garden City, N.Y.: Anchor Books, 1960.

ism can be granted, and its contributions to Western culture appreciated without an acceptance of medieval thought. Similarly, the results of the culture of the Enlightenment, seen as coming to flower in state education, can be recognized and accepted without a requisite assent to the underlying structure of thought.

What are some of the conspicuous results of the presently dying culture, and, in particular, of its schools?

First of all, by its studied rootlessness and its clean slate concept, it has clearly broken the back-bone of traditional Christianity, which now survives only as a peripheral, derivative and truncated structure. This is an achievement of no small merit. The reformers found their work soon overwhelmed, not only by the Enlightenment, but by traditionalism, Arminianism, and Pelagianism. The faith and doctrine of the church was more emasculated by its adherents than by its foes. Christianity today better commands the adherence rather than the allegiance of its followers, and its faith is so conditioned by the age as to be almost equally vulnerable with it. True Christianity today requires so radical a break with the church and Christianity at large, and with contemporary culture, as to be both an unpopular and limited force and yet able alone to break with the present culture in terms of a governing hope. The vested church today, by hurling its anathemas at its Machens, both writes its own death warrant and guarantees the creation of the church of the future. Epistemological self-consciousness is accelerated by the studied rootlessness of this era, and the groundwork prepared for cultural maturation. Since not all roots, religious, economic, familist or political, are of necessity good roots, the studied rootlessness of this dying era has been effective indeed in wiping the slate clean not only of defective Christianity but all its religious and secular rivals as well, all now floating insecurely on the floods of historical process.

Second, even as the Roman Empire created the conditions for cultural exchange and receptivity to Christianity from Britain to China by its peace and commerce, even at the moment of its sickness, so the modern culture has created an even wider condition of world-wide receptivity by its radical action on all existing cultures. The development of media of communication is no small contribution, but even greater has been the development of receptivity by the breakdown of past cultures. The 19th century saw an extensive development of missionary activity in areas newly impressed by Western superiority and ready to accept its religion as an aspect of that superiority. The effect of both westernization and modernized Christianity was to accelerate cultural decomposition, to aggravate old hostilities and create new ones as the traditional cushions against conflict were eroded. But, while mass man is thus being created on a world-wide scale, man still remains basically the God-created though fallen man, inescapably responsible for better or worse. The rising pressure of cultural decay will thus only intensify both the anxiety and receptivity of man and makes possible, for good or ill, the rise of a new culture. No better opportunity exists for a world-wide but pluralistic culture to develop.

Third, the culture of the Enlightenment has made no small contribution in destroying itself. By promulgating through education and in every other way possible its every standard of self-fulfilment as well as social unity, it has made possible its own death at the hands of its children. Liberty, fraternity, and equality, the reign of reason, deliverance from the past both historically and psychologically, the reign of a sovereign and messianic state, economic utopianism, the reign and freedom of love, human fulfilment in and through sex, all these and other ideals have been stridently proclaimed, only to end in frustration. Its own triumphs it has marred by its extravagant hopes, and thus prepared the way for its savage abandonment.

Fourth, but closely connected with the foregoing, the this-worldly orientation of the Enlightenment has been a necessary corrective to the unbiblical otherworldliness and spirituality of traditional Christianity and especially other religions. The bitter cynicism of "pies in the sky, by and by" religions has been wholesome in its effect and has required faith to be relevant. The biblical honesty of Abram, who felt blessing should be a present fact, was manifest in his frank question, "Lord God, what wilt thou give me, seeing I go childless?" (Gen. 15:2). Without agreeing with contemporary educational relativism, or its faith in easy answers, we can welcome its insistent restoration of the dimension of fulfilment to life, with this corrective, that the biblical faith offers not an *easy* life but rather a *good* one, as witness Psalm 23. The triumph of Christ's Kingdom has both its historical and eschatalogical aspects, and the dimension of fulfilment is a necessary aspect of Christan faith and cultural hope.

Fifth, the dominance of the church, and, outside Christianity, of pagan priests, and shamans, has been broken, an essential and healthy aspect of this culture. Although replaced now by the dominance of the state, this being a like evil, the dominance of the state is more vulnerable to cynicism and hence decay. The emergence of a truly pluralistic society, with cultural freedom and growth, requires the destruction of the claims of both church and state to be the Kingdom manifest. The degeneration of the Enlightenment into barren analysis has been destructive of the claims of every institution, church and state included.

Sixth, the humanism which developed out of the Enlightenment was both a reaction against Christianity and a product of it and, despite its very serious defects, was an important and significant cultural agent. While the culture of humanism has often meant the debasement of popular culture, the debasement is not all demerit by any means. The despised "dime-store" culture of today is a necessary and invaluable corollary of humanism, which is not necessarily anti-aristocratic and certainly conducive to a cultural law of supply and demand which is ultimately capable of more virile results. Humanism, by its emphasis on time as against eternity will of necessity lead its followers to a congeniality to the ephemeral. But the ephemeral is by no means necessarily to be despised, for to despise the ephemeral is to hate time and ultimately history. Cultural pyramid builders try futilely to negate time and only succeed in wasting it. The United States, as the epitome of humanistic culture and "dime store" living, is still the envy of the world for precisely these reasons. Cheap and disposable articles are manufactured, inadequate though lovely buildings torn down and replaced, not out of any contempt of culture but by a healthy respect for time, present time, and thus a respect for future time as well. In the long run, it will be manifest that the "ephemeral" culture of humanism has been more productive of "enduring" culture than its rivals and predecessors. Its wastes and mistakes are the luxury of experimentation, of trial and error, all evidences of freedom. In this emphasis on time, the public schools have been invaluable, not only in the extreme stress of progressive education on "preparation for life," but in basic education's insistence on a similar preparation for life by means of intellectual tools and skills. Moreover, the emphasis on time has not been the meaningless and directionless goal of Greek and Roman pessimism but an optimistic faith in the subordination of time and space to the fulfilment of man, an ideal of neo-Christian character and Christian derivation. Humanism, of course, has not exorcised all the cultural pyramid builders in its own ranks, as witness the Marxists, and, in every area, the extensive status-seeking lust, but this is indicative of the failure of humanism to give the dimension of identity and vocation provided by true Christianity, and, while a failure, does not detract from the importance of its restoration of the ephemeral to a place of dignity and meaning.

Seventh, technology is an important result of humanism and very clearly so. The emphasis on man and his fulfilment made it inevitable that man put knowledge and science to his service. Certainly, if the Sabbath was made for man and not man for the Sabbath, this is no less true of science, art, and all knowledge. Although the outcome has been the steady seizure of these things by the state, on the principle that man and his science is a creature of the state, even the state must do it in lip service to the humanist ideal, and knowledge and science are treated as instrumental to man's fulfilment. Technology has been made an inescapable fact of cultural activity and added a new dimension to man by liberating him from the limitations of his hands and immediate mental or physical activity. By instruments of computation and automation, man has become more fully man and added to his reach in every respect, added dimension to his life and living. While failing to give identity and meaning to man's added powers, the fact nonetheless remains that man has gained immeasurably by means of technology. To despise technology and its contributions is to despise life and time. Education has not only stimulated technology by creating a demand for it but also by gearing education to the furthering of man's subjugation of natural forces to human ends. In view of man's biblical mandate to subdue the earth in terms of his kingly office, such a result of contemporary education and culture is by no means to be despised but must be recognized as an imperative requirement of any true culture.

More could be said to indicate the important contributions of the Enlightenment and its cultural development, one of whose great monuments is the modern school. It has been a movement of tremendous power, sweeping across every continent in only a few centuries. Nonetheless, while in many respects a great liberating force, it has been also the source of the greatest actual and potential slavery history has yet known. By its agnostic secularism, it has become the fountainhead of tyranny. The vast dividing line between God's absolute and legislative authority and man's delegated and ministerial power has been dissolved, and the secular state made steadily the source of an absolutism exceeding God's own exercise of power. Rulers, presidents, senators, governors, and judges no longer sit in terms of a higher and transcendental law, government and court, but as law and authority incarnate. Hence the growing necessity that a president have the "father image," or a comparable significance, in that he carries now primarily the weight of final authority on his shoulders and must play god. A man stands now in front of judges who increasingly know no law beyond the state, and the man is thus helpless, both because the court is too closely identified with law and because secular man has less and less any faith in an appeal to Caesar's God. Relativism has thus robbed life of the dimension and perspective of God's absolute law and of the possibility of withstanding the demonic forces of history. Man's radical impotence is the outcome, in that no power above and beyond human power can arm or defend the oppressed man. Thus, the most demonic of all tyrannies is that which relativism produces, in that the assurance of hope and victory are undercut, and the dimension of fulfilment, never more clearly offered to man, becomes thus a sardonic mockery of his impotence. As Van Riessen has pointed out, "The *disintegration of existence,* i.e., the dissolution of coherence in the elements of existence, has reached an advanced stage for a great many people."[2]

In this disintegration of existence, the state schools have played an important part.[3] Man cannot live by bread alone, nor can he live by bread and ideas. How then does he or can he truly live? The answer of Jesus was clear-cut: "Man shall not live by bread alone, but by every word that proceedeth out of the mouth of God" (Matt. 4:4). The true circumstance of life is God and His word, and only in terms of this can man have identity and fulfilment. The miscellaneous tag ends of various cultures now taught, together with technology, as education, are not education but scraps from the educational table.

Again, the disintegration of existence, ironically running parallel with the radical improvement in the conditions of existence,

[2] H. Van Riessen: *The Society of the Future,* p. 225. Phila.: Presbyterian & Reformed Publ. Co., 1957.

[3] The term "public school" is no longer valid, public or common schools ante-dating the tax-supported, state-controlled schools, despite the continued use of this deceptive term. The schools today are government or state schools. "Parochial schools" are church-supported and church-controlled schools. "Private schools" are either secular schools operated and controlled by individuals or small corporations, or religiously oriented while similarly under private control. "Christian schools" or "Christian day schools" are anti-statist and anti-parochial and are operated by school associations of parents uniting to further education in terms of their basic faith and in integral relationship to the home, which is in a very real sense the sponsoring and supporting institution.

has been especially marked in the realm of the family. The decline and erosion of the Christian concept of the family is one of the most far-reaching tragedies of this era. As has been often pointed out, one of the points of radical cleavage between Christianity and the Roman Empire was the refusal of Christianity to see the church in Roman fashion as an aspect of the state, the function of religion then being the provision of social cement. The unity and absolutism of the state was thus broken, making possible the modern conception of liberty. The unity of life in the ancient world was a unity of a most dangerous nature. Religion was an aspect of the life of the state, in that the state, or its ruler, or some aspect of its being, was divine. Accordingly, every aspect of life, art, agriculture, commerce, everything, was an aspect of the life of the state. Religion, state and life were one. The temple, the butcher shop (or shambles), bank, labor guild and the family were all aspects of the life of the state, and the state was linked with the life of a god or company of gods. The societal and cosmic bond of heaven and earth, as set forth in the Tower of Babel and the Babylonian ziggurats,[4] was the characteristic feature of life in antiquity outside of Israel, and it was this unity which Christianity steadily destroyed (despite attempts of some churchmen to recreate it) and which now the modern state and school seek to re-establish. The unity of the ancient divinized state was a unity without transcendence, because the concept of continuity, the bond of heaven and earth, made time and eternity subject to a common life. The life of the gods, while superior, was not transcendent and lacked a radical discontinuity with the world of flux. Thus, the gods too were subject to defeat and eclipse, creatures themselves of mutability and decay. Thus, while the realm of the gods might on one hand be far greater in dignity and remoteness than that of Christian theology with its doctrine of the incarnation, on the other hand the realm of the

---

[4] See Eric Burrows, "Some Cosmological Patterns in Babylonian Religion," pp. 43-70 in S. H. Hooks, ed., *The Labyrinth,* Further Studies in the Relation between Myth and Ritual in the Ancient World, London, SPCK, 1935; and Andre Parrot: *The Tower of Babel,* N.Y. Philosophical Library, 1955.

gods was subject to the same law of change as the world of man, whereas for Christian theology the two realms can never be confused. The essence of this conflict, never understood by Gibbon but decisive to Western history, centered on the two natures of Christ. The definition of Chalcedon, 451, spoke of "our Lord Jesus Christ, at once complete in Godhead and complete in manhood, truly God and truly man." This Jesus Christ is

> of one substance with the Father as regards, his Godhead, and at the same time of one substance with us as regards his manhood; like us in all respects, apart from sin. . . . one and the same Christ, son, Lord, Only-begotten, recognized in TWO NATURES, WITHOUT CONFUSION, WITHOUT CHANGE, WITHOUT DIVISION, WITHOUT SEPARATION; the distinction of natures being in no way annulled by the union, but rather the characteristics of each nature being preserved and coming together to form one person and subsistence, not as parted or separated into two persons, but one and the same Son and Only-begotten God the Word, Lord Jesus Christ; even as the prophets from earliest times spoke of him, and our Lord Jesus Christ Himself taught us, and the creed of the Fathers has handed down to us.

The issue was all-important: to assert that the human can become the divine, that the eternal and temporal can inter-mingle, that time and eternity can have each an independent or co-equal existence, is to temporalize eternity and make it no longer determinative of time. Moreover, the temporal is then at fault only in that it is temporal, and the goal of man is seen in eternalizing himself and his order, in trying to create a church order or a social order which will freeze time into eternity, an ideal zealously pursued in medieval and modern no less than ancient times. The implications of Chalcedon are a denial of the validity of this. The weakness of man is not metaphysical, is not finitude, as ancients, scholastics, neo-orthodox, and existentialist thinkers would have it; it is ethical. It is not "the quest for certainty" man must renounce, but rather the very quest for eternity which Dewey himself sought in his "great community," the actualization of eternity in time, the achievement of a final order, the "end" of history. The denial of Chalcedon is the rejection of the determination of time by eternity together with a refusal to let time be time; it must be eternalized or at the very least arrested. The goal in every area of life becomes this contempt of time, expressed either idealistically or cynically. But, in the Christian sense, to respect eternity is to respect time. And such ability as early Christianity had in providing a new social order, in providing what William Carroll Bark has called the frontier thinking of that age, came with this sundering of the deadly unity of ancient culture, the bond of heaven and earth. It is this bond which made Babylon a type of all the opposition to God offered by man and Satan in *Revelation*. It was the attempt to overcome this sundering, with all its cultural implications, which marked the Christological controversy. The state-controlled churchmen, with their allegiance to an eternalized absolutism and a state-centered unity of time and eternity, were hostile to the attempt to force that separation. Chalcedon was thus a death sentence on the ancient world and the beginning of true liberty. Hellenic thought, however, within the Church of Rome, sought to re-establish the bond, and, as Scholasticism gives evidence, reintroduced the confusion. This Luther failed to purge from the Church, while Calvin again restored the significance of Chalcedon in this respect.[5] The effects of the Reformation are now rapidly being destroyed, and the State is again becoming the ancient unity of heaven and earth, the focus of life and meaning. It is both the ancient and new Leviathan, offering itself as the true opium of the masses, the source of all wealth, service, security, futurity and meaning.

Against all this, the Christianity which came to focus at Chalcedon made a radical stand, so that even Sozomen, writing a little earlier and coming from the more subservient East, could still affirm that the family belongs to God and not to the state.

[5] See C. Van Til: *The Metaphysics of Apologetics,* and R. J. Rushdoony: *By What Standard?*, pp. 19-64.

Such a concept was alien to a world which felt that the two were inseparable, that what belonged to the god of the State most certainly belonged to the State also. But today the sway of Chalcedon is disappearing, and all the gains it represented ignored, forgotten or despised. Abortion had been an early battle-line, pagan thinkers either opposing it as an infringement of state rights or defending it as necessary to the state. When opposed in terms of father-right by paganism, it was in terms of the religion of the group, i.e., ancestor worship, the veneration of the past and the solidarity of the social structure, rather than in terms of an absolute law. The argument of Christianity thus introduced a radical note, namely, that life belongs to God rather than to the social group. It is precisely this note that is now being submerged by the rise of statism. The structure of the family as an order from God and having certain rights beyond the state and its law is now disappearing, and education has been especially instrumental in its erosion. The Western family system has gone through a variety of changes in the past twenty centuries.[6] Now it faces not only its own decline but the disappearance of an order that will recognize its freedom; it is again being absorbed into a larger "family," the state conceived as the ultimate order of man. This state now possesses means to establish its power and dominion as never before. Liberty is thus no longer a God-given dimension of life but the area of toleration permissible to a state. And man, having no faith in any area of fulfilment other than the state, however much he may crave liberty from the state, is in actuality seeking merely license and escape, for freedom without faith becomes merely a desire for self-indulgence and an escape from responsibility. And the modern confusion of time and eternity makes a consistent and valid doctrine of liberty an impossibility. The disintegration of existence is, therefore, a product of that same confusion from whence Chalcedon once rescued a disintegrated world.

[6] See Carle C. Zimmerman: *Family and Civilization*, 1947, and *The Family of Tomorrow*, 1949, both published by Harpers.

When a world disintegrates, nothing more quickly becomes contemptible than its dead values, nothing more dead than its fallen gods, and nothing more offensively fetid than its old necessities. This will be no less true of the values of this dying age, of which one of the chiefest is the statist school. If the new order is capable of breaking with statism, it will in due course turn on every citadel of statism, the school no less than any other. At present, nothing seems more unlikely, although straws in the wind indicate the direction of the present temper. Government figures indicate that in the middle and late 1940's the state schools had 90% of the pupil population, with 10% in "private schools" of all classes. By 1959, the figures stood at 84% in state schools, and 16% in "private" schools. According to R. L. Hunt, "You can no longer take the public schools for granted" and he cites eight trends militating against such schools.[7]

But much more is involved. The state school is radically involved in the contemporary culture, both as a product thereof and its champion. In spite of adverse trends, it will survive as long as the culture survives, and no longer. To this culture, a compulsory state religion seems radically wrong, but not a compulsory state education. But between the two no real difference exists; both require the compulsive power of the state for whatever the culture deems necessary. Compulsion in religion was in an earlier era a social necessity, even as it now is in education. The cause of religion then required compulsion, even as the cause of education now requires compulsion and the state. In both instances, compulsion has been productive of very marked gains of a sort and of heavy penalties as well. But that education may play an even more important role in another age by no means requires that education be statist in even the slightest degree. Statist education will remain, for all the vehemence of the attacks on it, and will increase its reliance on and subservience to the

[7] R. L. Hunt, the National Council of Christian Churches, in a report, "Will Public Schools Survive?", summarized by Mark Fakkema in an article of the same title, part 1, in *The Christian Teacher*, Sept., 1959, p. 5 f.

state, as long as the contemporary culture remains, but, with the collapse of that culture, the education of that culture will rapidly wither away. And we are at the end of an age, in an era turning rapidly on itself and looking vainly thus far for a new sense of direction.

Such direction is requisite for new life and vitality. Long before the medieval culture gave way to another, its men were cynical and contemptuous of its values. Nevertheless, the over-all jurisdiction and authority of the church successfully survived the cynicism and only foundered against the rocks of new faiths. Despite their cynicism men could not think of a world apart from that church, and, indeed, some of the most biting of cynics, Erasmus included, required that world. So the modern concept of the over-all government and jurisdiction of the state will survive the bitterest resentment and cynicism as readily as did the church. It is not the satirists of the venality of priests or the frauds of tax assessors who can create a new culture, but only those who move, not in barren hostility, but in terms of an active faith which gives new ground and structure to society. "The hollow men" of T.S. Eliot now govern the world, and are its citizens also, all alike haunted by the sense of onrushing disaster, tormented by the pointlessness of life, and, in an age of scientific precision, given to a religious and philosophical vagueness and ambiguity. In art, love, religion and all of life, technique has become the substitute for meaning and an escape from reality. Lacking hope for the future, man also tries to destroy the past and its decisiveness, as witness Sartre.[8] What Levi calls Nietzsche's "will to illusion"[9] is the characteristic now of an age, one self-consciously dedicated to illusion.

The end of an age is always a time of turmoil, war, economic catastrophe, cynicism, lawlessness, and distress. But it is also an era of heightened challenge and creativity, and of intense vitality. And because of the intensification of issues, and their

[8] See Albert William Levi: *Philosophy and the Modern World*, p. 421. Bloomington, Indiana: Indiana U. Press, 1959.
[9] *Ibid.*, p. 40.

world-wide scope, never has an era faced a more demanding and exciting crisis. This then above all else is the great and glorious era to live in, a time of opportunity, one requiring fresh and vigorous thinking, indeed a glorious time to be alive.

Appendix 1

Academic Freedom

In recent years, academic authorities have, as in the past, found it necessary at times to censure or suppress student publications. This has occurred at state universities, Ivy colleges, and at Calvin College[1] as well. In each instance, some students, and occasionally a faculty member, have raised the cry of peril to academic freedom. The same protest has been raised when faculty members have been dismissed as Communists.

The whole controversy, in all its facets and instances, reveals an appalling ignorance of the meaning of freedom, a fact which is all the more unhappy when it occurs on a Christian college campus. For the true understanding of freedom is basically theological, and the fabric of liberty is progressively weakened as our culture loses its theological foundation. The kind of freedom commonly claimed by men in our day is not the freedom of the creature but the freedom of would-be gods. Properly speaking, God alone is free and beyond responsibility to anything or any-

[1] Calvin College is at Grand Rapids, Mich., and is sponsored by the Christian Reformed Church.

one other than Himself. The freedom of the creature is both limited and responsible. Man cannot fly, nor can he be born when he chooses, or with the face or abilities he selects. Neither can he ever act independently of God and man but must at all times act with responsibility. Above, beyond and over his will is the absolute and sovereign God, who "from all eternity did by the most wise and holy counsel of his own will, fully and unchangeably ordain whatsoever comes to pass." Nevertheless, God's decree does not offer violence "to the will of the creatures, nor is the liberty or contingency of second causes taken away, but rather established" (Westminster Confession, III, 1). The freedom of the creature is real only because of God's eternal decree, and it is never real except in terms of limitation and responsibility.

The significance of this becomes more understandable as we examine in turn political liberty, religious freedom, and academic freedom. The free political order recognizes liberty but within the jurisdiction of responsibility and limitation. Unlimited freedom, as in the Greek city-states, becomes tyranny wherein any group can enslave another or legislate at will because it has the capacity and liberty to do so. True political liberty establishes the restraint of law, insists on liability, cannot tolerate any creed which works to overthrow it, and will not confuse freedom of the press, for example, with freedom to libel or slander, but will impose restrictions to guarantee freedom with responsibility.

In like manner, religious liberty cannot be an unlimited freedom, nor does such religious liberty exist in the United States, nor is it guaranteed by law. There is no freedom granted to religious cults to indulge in such practices as infanticide, polygamy, human sacrifice, sexual rites, the burning of heretics, or other practices occurring in various religions. When, in the last century, the Mormon polygamists attempted to justify their multiple marriages on the constitutional ground of religious freedom, the Supreme Court was quick to point out that such unlimited freedom was an impossibility. Any and every practice could then be defended on the grounds of religious liberty. The Supreme Court has recognized only those practices as compatible with religious liberty in America which do not go against Christian standards. It admittedly recognized Christianity, not as a revealed or official religion, but as a common law faith determining the nature and limits of the law in the United States. Any total concept of religious liberty is an impossibility for the creature and for his society, and it has been in a true sense a product of Christian culture that constitutional or limited freedom has become a guiding principle of certain nations. And constitutional or limited liberty has been the most secure in its existence and results because it is more theologically valid.

The same principle applies to academic liberty. Properly speaking, there has been no instance in our generation in America of a violation of academic freedom. This term can only apply when scholars are denied the right of research and the right to publish or make known the result of honest and valid research. To apply the term academic freedom to anything else is to misuse it. It has, however, been misused by scholars who have viciously worked to undermine the basic standards of an institution while in its pay and ostensibly working to forward its concept of education. Academic freedom cannot be used to justify the teaching of communism in a state institution dedicated to the welfare of the free political order, nor can it be used to justify or defend the teaching of Buddhism or modernism in a Christian college. In like manner, students have a responsibility and a corresponding limitation to the educational institution as long as they are a part thereof and bear its name, in that the institutional character and reputation is involved in their conduct. Admittedly, this limitation can be abused, but the actual fact is that most institutions, including Christian colleges, have leaned over backwards to show respect to the expression of the students even when it has been a source of serious trouble to them. For this forbearance, they are to be commended if it is based on a healthy respect for true Christian liberty rather than a tolerance without principle.

When the students of Calvin College, through the *Chimes* protest the withdrawal of the *Literary Review* in the name of academic freedom, they show a singular ignorance of the meaning of creaturely liberty, and irresponsibility as well. An honest but still kindly verdict on the *Literary Review* would be that it is almost consistently poor and immature writing which is secular in spirit. Its secularity is a reflection both on the students and the school. Christian writing does not require a use of religious terminology or subjects, but it does involve a consistently Christian purpose. The failure of the *Chimes* to understand the meaning of freedom is especially striking. In a Calvinist institution, of all places, the exercise of freedom should be seen in terms of the responsibility and limitations of the creature under God, rather than a rebellious son of Adam seeking to be a god and denouncing all of God's and man's just requirements of him. This lack of understanding is a theological failure that reflects on both the students and the faculty and requires challenging.

Appendix 2

The Menace of the Sunday School

It is always easier to see the splinter in another's eye than the beam in our own. It is likewise easier for Christians to see the sins of the world than the sins of the church. Each theological faction grabs readily at the sins of others and fails to see their's.

But perhaps nowhere is the blindness more consistently seen than with regard to the Sunday School. Christianity knows perhaps no greater or more subtle menace. When one considers the tremendous investment of time and money which the Sunday School involves, the problem becomes all the more serious.

The Sunday School has its ready defenders, from J. Edgar Hoover on up and down. Judges and law enforcement officials generally join with the clergy in stating that children who attend Sunday School regularly are rarely involved in delinquency, and that the vast majority of criminals are enlistments from outside the ranks of the church. These statements are, moreover, true, and only serve to point up more sharply the essence of the problem.

The Sunday School is successful today in fostering a moral

citizenry. It constitutes a powerful weapon for social order and decency. It is a consistently effective weapon in combating juvenile delinquency. Law enforcement officials are right in their evaluation of the Sunday School's social value and function. With all this we have no quarrel.

We cannot and do not object to morality; it is a fitting and proper outcome of the Sunday School program, but we can and must call attention to the fact that the Sunday School is productive not only of morality but moralism. The liberal Sunday school program tends to reduce religion to moralism. The fundamentalist Sunday School identifies at times religion and moralism, or adds moralism to religion as a faith and works program for salvation.

A young woman, struggling with serious personal problems, confided to her pastor that her marital and personal failures had been compounded by her Sunday School training. A product of both liberal and fundamentalist churches, she stated that everything she ever learned in Sunday School insisted that she had to be good to be a Christian, while everything she had now learned most emphatically declared that she was a Christian, not because she was good, but because God is good, that not her righteousness but God's righteousness saved her and was the foundation of her daily life. The first attitude had led her into a reasonable, kindly but still clearly self-righteous life, one in which her handling of problems depended on her works. The second attitude gave her a recognition of her nature as a sinner saved by grace and a dawning, joyful humility and dependence on God which began to offer hope for a solution of her problems. In her moralistic frame of mind, she had been unable to accept herself or life; she was filled with doubts and frustrations. In her godly frame of mind, she accepted herself and life with a growing realism and a growing recognition that she had to see herself as God saw her, to be ready to accept His love and recognize the honor and glory it gave her, and grow in terms of it.

This incident brings to focus the menace of the Sunday School. It teaches precisely that faith which the pulpit is called upon to wage war against. It inculcates either outright Pelagianism and works-salvation, as in liberal circles, or a judaizing faith in conservative circles. Its effects are almost invariably moralistic. Although some lesson materials clearly emphasize the gospel, the greater majority of teachers even more clearly teach the children that they must be good like Jesus wants them to be, and avoid being bad. Such teaching is a standing offense to the godly pulpit and to Scripture. It is subversive of all Christianity. The fact that in some Sunday Schools salvation is taught and decisions called for does not alter the facts; atonement and the cross are added on to goodness and works as the means of salvation, and this is the practical effect on the minds of the pupils. Virtually every Sunday School youngster can give some kind of definition of what good and bad mean, but not one in ten thousand can define the covenant of grace.

Another unhappy fact must be noted. Because of its moralistic nature, the Sunday School attracts as teachers a very high proportion of "do-gooders," people whose delight it is to participate in every kind of community activity and who glow with civic and moral righteousness because they do so. Because of their deep-seated moralism, they tend to under-rate the services of divine worship and make more important the Sunday School program. Family attendance at church services has given way to a priority for children's attendance at Sunday School. Because worship is equated with understanding alone, a moralistic equation, it is asserted that children are better off in Sunday School, junior church, or the nursery. It is not surprising that children who are trained in Sunday School attendance drift out of the church after school years, to return only when they have children to bring to Sunday School. The church school has become for them the central institution, and moralism their religion. They participate in the church in order to perpetuate the school. The Sunday School has become the triumph of the Sadducces and Pharisees, and the Judaizers as well. Sometimes it can only be described as anti-Christian. The pastor who prepares a sermon for Sunday morning and evening delivery on the meaning of Christian faith and life is struggling not only against the faith of the world but the faith of his own Sunday School.

What the children receive from the school, therefore, is not a godly faith but a moral faith, and the only consequences of such a development can be religious disaster. If Scripture means anything, it makes clear that God is very jealous of His honor, nor will He tolerate sacrilege. And the modern Sunday School program is sacrilegious in that its emphasis is not God but moralism and its results assessed too often in terms of happy social consequences rather than godliness. And whenever and wherever the Sunday School exists on this basis to any degree, it is a menace to Christianity and an offense to God.

Appendix 3

Coercion and the Christian School

The Christian school is not to be confused with a parochial school, in that it is not an adjunct of the church but the creation of an independent school society, formed by interested parents in terms of particular Christian and educational standards. Various church bodies have, however, taken an active interest in furthering and promoting the school as a matter of principle and in the firm and worthy conviction that the child is the responsibility, not of the state, but of the parents. The churches have felt so strongly about this, that they have felt it their responsibility to remind parents that children do not belong to Caesar, and that statist education is ultimately anti-Christian.

All this is excellent, but the problem arises as some churches exert an element of coercion on parents to further attendance. There is no disciplinary or coercive action taken by the church, but some pressure by the officers on the families to enter their children in the Christian school. In some instances, churches report to their official bodies the percentage of families whose children are entered in the Christian school, very often 100%.

While the *teaching* aspect is the valid and necessary responsibility of the church, i.e., to instruct parents in the implications of statist education and of godly education, the *recruitment* or *enlistment* is entirely the function of the school society. The greater majority are clearly in favor of Christian education; the minority usually fret, and then go along because of social pressure, fretting because of their unwillingness to bear a double load, the public schools through taxes, and the Christian school in tuition.

These unwilling parents become a drag on the school society. Anxious to keep down expenses, they are niggardly and grudging in financial matters, always faintly hostile but not honest enough to say why. As a result, the school society, although in some instances having a wealthy constituency, finds itself with limited funds and teachers underpaid, simply because an unhappy minority, unwilling to oppose a pastor and church officers, chooses to take it out on the school instead. The school society, as a voluntary organization, operates on a radically more economical basis than the public school in building, operational, administrative, and maintenance costs. On this basis it can still produce superior results. But, if even in a small measure, the principle of coercion enter into the Christian school, its basic strength is compromised.

The school society, through its parent members, is the best agency for recruitment. To maintain the integrity, vitality and strength of the society, unconvinced or unwilling members need to be dropped. The actively interested parents are often members who contribute over and above their tuition fees in order that other children may be included in the school. They are ready to give time and money to the furtherance of the school in every aspect of its functions. Of themselves, they are capable of producing and do produce a strong school and an advanced standard of education. While the unhappiness of those who fret at a double taxation is understandable, their presence in the school society is detrimental and can undercut the strength of the Christian school.

This has often been the case. In some schools, excellent

teachers have become discouraged at their failure to make enough to live on and have been compelled to resign, and capable and dedicated parents have become discouraged at their difficulty in furthering something so zealously begun. The interference of the church on behalf of the school brings an *increase* to the school, but does not *prosper* it. Both for the school and the church, the results will be better if the element of pressure is completely eliminated by the church. A parent ready to make concession to statist education is no gain to a school society, and its existence is to him in a sense a luxury, not a necessity. If, as the Christian school maintains, it is an independent domain and separate from state and church and an expression of Christian society and most closely linked with the family, then it must maintain its independence or surrender its integrity. This by no means precludes close ties with the institutional church, but it does preclude a subsidiary status.

In any society, great or small, as the measure of coercion rises, the sense of responsibility diminishes. As men find themselves able to surrender authority to state, church, or school, both their irresponsibility increases, and their complaints. Very often, in authoritarian societies, cynical humor, complaining and bickering is irresponsible man's only way of asserting his superiority to the foolish authorities without assuming any share of responsibility himself. Such cynicism and complaining exists, not as true protest, but as a form of compliance. It is not a sign of health, but of radical sickness. Neither educators nor churchmen can hope to gain respect if they create such a coercive situation, nor can they hope to further responsibility.

On the other hand, the independence of the Christian school cannot be read as the self-sufficiency of the school in the matters of government. The school cannot be the servant of the home; it is itself a manifestation also of the Kingdom. But neither can it create an independent hierarchy and deny the rights of parents. Sphere sovereignty is not sphere autonomy, and independence in any healthy sense means interdependence also.

Appendix 4

The Flesh and Bones of the Child

In his delightful autobiography, Dr. A. Nakashian describes his boyhood in Armenia, and his schooling. Education was of a limited sort, and difficult because of the restrictions imposed by the Turks. Other writers have described the difficulties experienced with the government; for example, a textbook in chemistry was once seized as revolutionary literature in code. The Turkish authorities were certain of proof in spotting the formula H_2O. The H_2 obviously referred to Abdul Hamid II, and the O, zero, meant he was to be assassinated.

Nakashian's mother took him to school and entrusted him to the teacher with the words, "His flesh is yours, but the bones are mine." (A. Nakashian: *A Man Who Found a Country*, p. 9. New York: Crowell, 1940.) This proverb, commonly used, had a double significance. First, it gave the teacher authority to teach and discipline the child. The child belonged to the parents, but the parents thereby delegated authority to the teacher. Second, it gave the flesh to the teacher to be molded or beaten as necessary, but with the bones, the basic structure, remaining the parents'.

126

Such education, while often seriously faulty, had still a healthy premise in that it did not assume the right to *re-make* the child, but rather sought to develop him in terms of the family's and society's culture. Modern education is increasingly careless of the flesh but claims the bones of the child, i.e., the right to re-create the child in its own image. When the school is given the flesh but not the bones, the school serves as a cultural agency and limits its function to education. When the school claims the bones, it declares that right belongs to the school and pre-empts the function of home and church.

Appendix 5

Montgomery's *School Question*

In 1886, Zach. Montgomery, assistant attorney-general of the United States, published his educational views, *The School Question*. A native of Kentucky and a resident of California, Montgomery for years waged a strenuous and able campaign against statist education, and a brief review of his arguments is of historical value.

His approach had three main aspects. First, he carefully developed the statistical argument, declaring that a correlation existed between statist education and the rise of delinquency, criminality, and suicide. States which had last gone over to "public" schools showed a low rate in each instance. He commented on the situation in New York as reported in 1881 by the United States Commissioner of Education, "From this statement it would appear that the *cost* of public-school work in the State of New York increases in an *inverse* ratio to the number of pupils taught, while, as we have seen, *crime increases in direct proportion to such cost.*"[1]

[1] Zach. Montgomery: *The School Question*, p. 25. Washington: Gibson, 1886.

128

Second, Montgomery challenged the right of the state to enter into the field of education, in that this was a parental concern. The children did not belong to the state, and the implications of statist education were definitely that they did, and Montgomery quoted educators to that effect. Montgomery felt that "there is no kind or degree of communism so utterly revolting as that which, for educational purposes, virtually asserts a community of title, not only to the property, but also to the children of the private citizen. Yet, this unfortunately, is the communism of America; a communism having for its main trunk an educational system the most ruinously expensive and the most demoralizing that the world ever saw."[2] Montgomery was fearful of the implications of the developing statism. He called attention to the changes in definitions of such words as "constitution," "union," and "federal" in Webster's Dictionary from 1859 to 1886. In 1859, for example, Webster defined "constitution" thus:

> In free States the Constitution is paramount to the statutes or laws enacted by the Legislature, limiting and controlling its power; and in the United States the Legislature is created and its powers designated by the Constitution.

By 1886, this definition had been completely discarded for a radically different one:

> The principal or fundamental laws which govern a State or other organized body of men, and are embodied in its written documents or implied in the institutions or usages of the country or society.

In terms of this amended definition, Montgomery observed, "the rising generation no longer look upon the written Constitution as the source and limit of legislative power; but on the contrary the mere 'usages of society' are raised to the dignity of constitutional law."[3]

Third, Montgomery believed in 'private' education as the

[2] *Ibid.,* p. 133.
[3] *Ibid.,* p. 38 f.

means of furthering the life of state, church and school. Although a Roman Catholic, he was militantly opposed to any attempt by that church, or any church, to secure public funds for parochial or private schools, in that this was as statist a course as outright state schools, in that it implied that the children were the state's concern and belonged to the state rather than parents.

> We utterly deny that the State *has* any children. It is true that, by a fiction of the law in use in England, *bastard* children are sometimes called the children of the people. And if . . (one) intends to say that the property of the State should bear this burden of educating the State's bastard children, we shall urge no particular objection; but then the question arises, What *is* the property of the State? Surely it is not the property of the private citizen. If the State owns all the property which we have heretofore supposed belonged to individual citizens, the reign of Communism has already begun. If, as seems to be claimed, the State owns all the children and all the property too, we can see no good reason why she may not, and ought not, in common fairness, to make an equal distribution of her own property amongst her own children. After all, this is the true theory upon which rests this Communistic system of public schools.[4]

Lest some argue that in an enlightened or Christian state these dangers were not as real, nor limitations as necessary, as in pagan or pre-Christian societies, Montgomery made it clear that Christianity gave no new right to the state, nor any additional powers, and that no pagan prince ever gained any new right over his subjects by baptism.[5]

An attempt was made by Senator Ingalls of Kansas to block Montgomery's appointment in view of these opinions, but the move failed thoroughly, and he served during Grover Cleveland's administration. The issues with regard to education were not as clear-cut in Montgomery's day, in that local control of schools was still so strong and transportation so slow that the state and

[4] *Ibid.*, p. 46 f.
[5] *Ibid.*, p. 47 ff.

its power sometimes seemed very remote. Thus, while he had extensive support, his effort failed; in the minds of too many people, the implications of statism were not yet sufficiently apparent for the warning to seem other than alarmist.

Appendix 6

Biblical Justice

Since there are many who confuse the concepts of poetic justice with the biblical doctrine of justice, it is advisable, briefly, to call attention to an essential aspect of the difference. Poetic justice is an impersonal law which automatically and assuredly rights every wrong and avenges every evil. Biblical justice is personal and rests on the nature of the triune God. Unless a man find atonement in Christ, strict retribution prevails, so that "every idle word that men shall speak, they shall give account thereof in the day of judgment" (Matt. 12:36). While Scripture gives extensive evidence of God's avenging justice in history, and the Book of Revelation affirms that fact emphatically, it should be noted that the tribunal is not history, but "the day of judgment." Not only poetic justice, but other attempts as well to derive a concept of justice from nature, founder on this appeal to history. However valid the evidence deduced, it still leaves a cold and impersonal doctrine of justice, against which men ultimately rebel in favor of antinomian concepts. The appeal to history characterizes every false concept of justice, whereas the biblical doctrine, by its appeal to God and its foundation in His infallible Word, is a transcendental concept with biblical and general historical exemplification.

Poetic justice, moreover, requires historical movement in terms of a single end, the fulfilment of justice, whereas biblical justice is set in the context of a multitude of strands in every situation, all involved in God's total and providential government. Thus, from the human point of view, God's justice is often characterized by great delay, but not so from the biblical perspective. The totality of God's purpose is always operative, and justice, an aspect of that totality, finds fulfilment only in terms of the totality, whose scope reaches far beyond the immediate or even the historical perspective.